D0502536

INTELLECTUAL MEMOIRS

NEW YORK 1936-1938

Books by Mary McCarthy

THE COMPANY SHE KEEPS

THE OASIS

CAST A COLD EYE

THE GROVES OF ACADEME

A CHARMED LIFE

MEMORIES OF A CATHOLIC GIRLHOOD

VENICE OBSERVED

THE STONES OF FLORENCE

ON THE CONTRARY

THE GROUP

MARY McCARTHY'S THEATRE CHRONICLES

THE WRITING ON THE WALL

BIRDS OF AMERICA

THE SEVENTEENTH DEGREE

THE MASK OF STATE: WATERGATE PORTRAITS

CANNIBALS AND MISSIONARIES

IDEAS AND THE NOVEL

OCCASIONAL PROSE

HOW I GREW

INTELLECTUAL MEMOIRS

MARY McCARTHY

INTELLECTUAL
MEMOIRS

NEW YORK 1936-1938

WITH A FOREWORD BY
ELIZABETH HARDWICK

HARCOURT BRACE JOVANOVICH, PUBLISHERS
NEW YORK   SAN DIEGO   LONDON

HBJ

Requests for permission to make copies of any
part of the work should be mailed to:
Permissions Department, Harcourt Brace Jovanovich, Publishers,
8th Floor, Orlando, Florida 32887.

Portions of this book have appeared in the *Paris Review, Granta,* and
Interview.

Library of Congress Cataloging-in-Publication Data
McCarthy, Mary, 1912–
Intellectual memoirs: New York 1936–1938/Mary McCarthy;
with a foreword by Elizabeth Hardwick.—1st ed.
p.   cm.
ISBN 0-15-144820-5
1. McCarthy, Mary, 1912–   —Homes and haunts—New York
(N.Y.) 2. New York (N.Y.)—Intellectual life—20th century.
3. Authors, American—20th century—Biography. I. Title.
PS3525.A1435Z47   1992
818'.520—dc20   91-40333

Designed by Lydia D'moch

Printed in the United States of America

First edition
A B C D E

FOREWORD

Intellectual Memoirs: New York 1936–1938. I look at the title of these vivid pages and calculate that Mary McCarthy was only twenty-four years old when the events of this period began. The pages are a continuation of the first volume, to which she gave the title: *How I Grew.* Sometimes with a sigh she would refer to the years ahead in her autobiography as "I seem to be embarked on how I grew and grew and grew." I am not certain how many volumes she planned, but I had the idea she meant to go right down the line, inspecting the troops you might say, noting the slouches and the good soldiers and, of course, inspecting herself living in her time.

Here she is at the age of twenty-four, visiting the memory of it, but she was in her seventies when the actual writing was accomplished. The arithmetic at both ends is astonishing. First, her electrifying ("to excite intensely or suddenly as if by electric shock") descent upon New York City just after her graduation from Vassar College. And then after more than twenty works of fiction, essays, cultural and political commentary, the defiant perseverance at the end when she was struck by an unfair series of illnesses, one after another. She bore these afflictions with a gallantry that was almost a disbelief, *her* disbelief, bore them with a high measure of hopefulness, that sometime companion in adversity that came not only from the treasure of consciousness but also, in her case, from an acute love of *being there* to witness the bizarre motions of history and the also, often, bizarre intellectual responses to them.

Intellectual responses are known as opinions and Mary had them and had them. Still she was so little of an ideologue as to be sometimes unsettling in her refusal of tribal reaction—left or right, male or female, that sort of thing. She was doggedly personal and often this meant being so aslant that there was, in this determined rationalist, an endearing crankiness, very American and homespun somehow. This was true especially in domestic matters, which held a high place in her life. There she is grinding the coffee beans of a morning in a wonderful wooden and iron contraption that seemed to me designed for muscle-building—a workout it was. In her acceptance speech upon receiving the MacDowell Colony Medal for Literature she said that she did not *believe* in laborsaving devices. And thus she kept on year after year, up to her last days, clacking away on her old green Hermes nonelectric typewriter, with a feeling that this effort and the others were akin to the genuine in the arts—to the handmade.

I did not meet Mary until a decade or so after the years she writes about in this part of her autobiographical calendar. But I did come to know her well and to know most of the "characters," if that is the right word for the friends, lovers, husbands, and colleagues who made up her cast after divorce from her first husband and the diversion of the second John, last name Porter, whom she did not marry. I also lived through much of the cultural and political background of the time, although I can understand the question asked, shyly, by a younger woman writing a biography of Mary: "Just what is a Trotskyite?" Trotskyite and Stalinist—part of one's descriptive vocabulary, like blue-eyed. Trotsky, exiled by Stalin and assassinated in Mexico in 1940, attracted leftists, many of them with Socialist leanings, in opposition to the Stalin of the Moscow Trials, beginning in 1936, which ended in the execution of most of the original Bolsheviks and the terror that followed.

The preoccupation with the Soviet Union, which lasted, with violent mutations of emphasis, until just

about yesterday, was a cultural and philosophical bat-
tleground in the years of Mary McCarthy's "debut"
and in the founding, or refounding, of the magazine
Partisan Review. In that circle, the Soviet Union, the
Civil War in Spain, Hitler and Mussolini, were what
you might call real life but not in the magazine's pages
more real, more apposite, than T. S. Eliot, Henry
James, Kafka, and Dostoyevski.

The memoir is partly "ideas" and very much an
account of those institutional rites that used to be re-
corded in the family Bible: marriage, children, divorce,
and so on. Mary had only one child, her son, Reuel
Wilson, but she had quite a lot of the other rites: four
marriages, interspersed with love affairs of some seriousness and others of none. Far from taking the au-
tobiographer's right to be selective about waking up
in this bed or that, she tempts one to say that she
remembers more than scrupulosity demands—demands of the rest of us at least as we look back on
the insupportable surrenders and dim our recollection
with the aid of the merciful censor.

On the other hand, what often seemed to be at
stake in Mary's writing and in her way of looking at
things was a somewhat obsessional concern for the
integrity of sheer fact in matters both trivial and striking. "The world of fact, of figures even, of statis-
tics . . . the empirical element in life . . . the fetishism
of fact . . .": phrases taken from her essay "The Fact
in Fiction" (1960). The facts of the matter are the truth,

as in a court case that tries to circumvent vague feelings and intuitions. If one would sometimes take the liberty of suggesting caution to her, advising prudence or mere practicality, she would look puzzled and answer: but it's the truth. I do not think she would have agreed it was only *her* truth—instead she often said she looked upon her writing as a mirror.

And thus she will write about her life under the command to put it all down. Even the name of the real man in the Brooks Brothers shirt in the fiction of the same name, but scarcely thought by anyone to be a fiction. So at last, and for the first time, she says, he becomes a fact named George Black, who lived in a suburb of Pittsburgh and belonged to the Duquesne Club. As in the story, he appeared again and wanted to rescue her from New York bohemian life, but inevitably he was an embarrassment. As such recapitulations are likely to be: Dickens with horror meeting the model for Dora in later life. Little Dora of *David Copperfield*: "What a form she had, what a face she had, what a graceful, variable, enchanting manner!" Of course, the man in the Brooks Brothers shirt did not occasion such affirmative adjectives but was examined throughout with a skeptical and subversive eye. About the young woman, the author herself more or less, more rather than less, she would write among many other thoughts: "It was not difficult, after all, to be the prettiest girl at a party for the share-croppers."

The early stories in *The Company She Keeps* could,

for once, rightly be called a sensation: they were indeed a sensation for candor, for the brilliant lightning flashes of wit, for the bravado, the confidence, and the splendor of the prose style. They are often about the clash of theory and practice, taste and ideology. Rich as they are in period details, they transcend the issues, the brand names, the intellectual fads. In "The Portrait of the Intellectual as a Yale Man," we have the conflict between abstract ideas and self-advancement, between probity and the wish to embrace the new and fashionable. About a young couple, she writes: "Every social assertion Nancy and Jim made carried its own negation with it, like an Hegelian thesis. Thus it was always being said by Nancy that someone was a Communist but a terribly nice man, while Jim was remarking that someone else worked for Young and Rubicam but was astonishingly liberal."

In the memoir, we learn that we can thank Edmund Wilson for turning the young Mary away from writing reviews to undertaking fiction and thereby producing these dazzling stories. We also learn that she thanks him for little else. A good deal of these pages left at her death tell about her affair with Philip Rahv and *analyze* the break, in fact a desertion, from him and her marriage to Wilson. I must say that much of this drama was new to me. I was not in New York at the time. I met Mary for the first time in the middle 1940s when I was invited to Philip Rahv's apartment. She was with a young man who was to be her next husband after the "escape" from Wilson; that is, she was with Bowden Broadwater. Philip was married to Nathalie Swan, Mary's good friend from Vassar . . . A lot of water had flowed by.

The picture of Mary and Philip Rahv living in a borrowed apartment on East End Avenue, a fashionable street over by the wrong river since Philip was very much a downtown figure, rambling round the streets of Greenwich Village with a proprietary glance here and there for the tousled heads of Sidney Hook or Meyer Shapiro and a few others whom he called "luftmenschen." The memory, no matter the inevitable strains of difference between them, has an idyllic accent and she appears to have discovered in the writing, decades later, that she loved Rahv. There was to be an expulsion from the garden when Edmund Wilson met Mary, pursued her, and finally, a not very long "finally," got her to marry him.

The account of the moral struggle is a most curious and interesting one, an entangled conflict between inclination and obligation; the inclination to stay with Rahv and the obligation to herself, her principles, incurred when she got drunk and slept with Wilson and therefore had to marry him. The most engaging part of this struggle is not its credibility or inner consistency but the fact that Mary believed it to be the truth. There was a certain Jesuitical aspect to her moral life which for me was part of her originality and one of the outstanding charms of her presence. Very little was offhand; habits, prejudices, moments, even fleeting ones, had to be accounted for, looked at, and written in the ledger. I sometimes thought she felt the command to prepare and serve a first course at dinner ought to be put in the Bill of Rights.

I remember telling her about some offensive behavior to me on the part of people who were not her friends but mere acquaintances, if that. When she saw them on the street up in Maine she would faithfully "cut them"—a phrase she sometimes used—while I, when her back was turned, would be waving from the car. Yet it must be said that Mary was usually concerned to make up with those she had offended in fiction, where they were amusingly trapped in their peculiarities, recognizable, in their little ways, not to mention their large ways. Among these were Philip and Nathalie Rahv, whom she had wounded, painfully for them, in a novella, *The Oasis*. They too made up, after a time, after a time.

Details, details. Consider the concreteness of the apartments, the clothes, the inquisitive, entranced observing that had something in it of the Goncourt brothers putting it all down in the Paris of the second half of the nineteenth century. They will write: "On today's bill of fare in the restaurants we have authentic buffalo, antelope, and Kangaroo." There it is, if not quite as arresting as Flaubert making love in a brothel with his hat on. Mary remembers from the long-flown years that they on a certain occasion drank "Singapore Slingers." And the minutiae of her first apartment in

New York: "We had bought ourselves a tall 'modernistic' Russel Wright cocktail shaker made of aluminum with a wood top, a chromium hors d'oeuvres tray with glass dishes (using industrial materials was the idea), and six silver Old-Fashioned spoons with a simulated cherry at one end and the bottom of the spoon flat, for crushing sugar and Angostura." The cocktail age, how menacing and beguiling to the sweet tooth, a sort of liquid mugger.

Unlike the Goncourts' rather mad nocturnal stenography to fill their incomparable pages, I don't think Mary kept a diary. At least I never heard mention of one nor felt the chill on rash spontaneity that such an activity from this shrewdly observing friend would cast upon an evening. From these pages and from the previous volume, it appears that she must have kept clippings, letters certainly, playbills, school albums, and made use of minor research to get it right—to be sure the young man in Seattle played on the football team. In these years of her life, she treasured who was in such and such a play seen in an exact theater. On the whole, though, I believe the scene setting, the action, the dialogue, came from memory. These memories, pleasing and interesting to me at every turn, are a bit of history of the times. Going to *Pins and Needles*, the Federal Theater's tribute to the Ladies' Garment Workers' Union, a plain little musical with fewer of the contemporary theater's special effects than a performance of the church choir.

The pages of this memoir represent the beginning

of Mary McCarthy's literary life. She was a prodigy from the first. I remember coming across an early review when I was doing some work in the New York Public Library. It was dazzling, a wonderfully accomplished composition, written soon after she left college. As she began, so she continued, and in the years ahead I don't think she changed very much. There was a large circle of friends in France, England, and Italy as well as here at home, but Mary was too eccentric in her tastes to be called snobbish and I would not find her an especially worldly person. She was not fashionable so much as discriminating; but beyond it all there was the sentimental and romantic streak in her nature that cast a sort of girlish glow over private and public arrangements.

Year in and year out, she made fantastical demands on her time and her budget for birthdays, Christmas; presents, banquets, bouquets, surprises, a whole salmon for the Fourth of July, traditional offering. I remember Natasha Nabokov, the mother of Ivan Nabokov, a publisher in Paris, telling me of a Thanksgiving in Paris where Mary found an approximation of the American turkey and brought forth "two dressings, one chestnut and one oyster." Keeping the faith, it was. I often thought the holiday calendar was a command like the liturgical calendar with its dates and observances. Perhaps it was being an orphan, both of her parents having died in the flu epidemic of 1918, that led her to put such unusual stress on the reproduction of "family" gatherings.

Here she speaks of her "patrician" background, a word I never heard her use about herself. It was true that she came from the upper middle class, lawyers and so on, but all of it had been lived so far away in Minnesota and the state of Washington that one never thought of her as Middlewestern or Western but instead as American as one can be without any particularity of region or class. In any case, she created even in small, unpromising apartments a sort of miniature *haute bourgeois* scenery, without being imitative. And she would arrive in New York with Mark Cross leather luggage, a burdensome weight even when empty, pairs of white leather gloves, a rolled umbrella, all of it bringing to mind ladies of a previous generation—and no thought of convenience. Of course, she didn't believe in convenience.

Wide friendships and hospitality, yes, but there were, in my view, only two persons outside the family circle for whom she felt a kind of reverence. The two were Hannah Arendt and Nicola Chiaramonte, both Europeans. They met for Mary every standard of intellectual and moral integrity. Chiaramonte, a beautiful man with dark curls and brown (I think) eyes, was a curiosity in the *Partisan* circle because of his great modesty and the moderation of his voice in discussion, a gentle word for what was usually a cacophony of argument. An evening at the Rahvs was to enter a ring of bullies, each one bullying the other. In that way it was different from the boarding school accounts of the type, since no one was in ascendance. Instead there was an equality of vehemence that exhausted itself and the wicked bottles of Four Roses whiskey around midnight—until the next time. Chiaramonte, with his peaceable, anarchist inclinations, was outclassed here.

I suppose he could be called a refugee, this Italian cultural and social critic and anti-Fascist. Here he published essays but did not create a literary presence equal to his important career when he returned to Italy in the late 1940s. After his death, Mary wrote a long, interesting essay in order to introduce an American edition of his writings on the theater. I remember an anecdote she told me about Chiaramonte, and it alone is sufficient to show why she so greatly admired him. The story went as follows: stopped at a border, trying to escape the Nazi drive across Europe, Nicola was asked for his passport and he replied: Do you want the real one or the false one?

Hannah Arendt, of course, was or became an international figure with *The Origins of Totalitarianism, Eichmann in Jerusalem,* and other works. I can remember Mary at Hannah's apartment on Riverside Drive, a setting that was candidly practical, a neat place, tending toward a mute shade of beige in its appointments. For an occasional gathering there would be drinks and coffee and, German style it seemed to us, cakes and chocolates and nuts bought in abundance at the bakeries on Broadway. Mary was, quite literally, enchanted by Hannah's mind, her scholarship, her industry, and the complexities of her views. As for

Hannah, I think perhaps she saw Mary as a golden American friend, perhaps the best the country could produce, with a bit of our western states in her, a bit of the Roman Catholic, a Latin student, and a sort of New World, blue-stocking *salonière* like Rachel Varnhagen, about whom Hannah had, in her early years, written a stunning, unexpected book. The friendship of these two women was very moving to observe in its purity of respect and affection. After Hannah's death, Mary's extraordinary efforts to see her friend's unfinished work on questions of traditional philosophy brought to publication, the added labor of estate executor, could only be called sacrificial.

I gave the address at the MacDowell Colony when Mary received the Medal and there I said that if she was, in her writing, sometimes a scourge, a Savonarola, she was a very cheerful one, lighthearted and even optimistic. I could not find in her work a trace of despair and alienation; instead she had a dreamy expectation that persons and nations should do their best. Perhaps it would be unlikely that a nature of such exceptional energy could act out alienation, with its temptation to sloth. Indeed it seemed to me that Mary did not understand even the practical usefulness of an occasional resort to the devious. Her indiscretions were always open and forthright and in many ways one could say she was "like an open book." Of course, everything interesting depends upon which book is open.

Among the many charms and interests of this unfinished memoir are the accounts of the volatility of
her relations with the men in her life. She will say that
she doesn't know why she left her first husband, backed
out on John Porter, and deserted Philip Rahv. That is,
she doesn't know *exactly* but can only speculate. What,
perhaps, might be asked nowadays is why the gifted
and beautiful young woman was so greatly attracted
to marriage in the first place, why she married at
twenty-one. She seemed swiftly to overlook the con-
siderable difficulties of unmarried couples "living together" at the time: the subterfuge about staying
overnight, facing the elevator man, hiding the im-
pugning clothes when certain people appeared, keeping the mate off the phone lest there be a call from
home—unimaginable strategies in the present-day cities. There were many things Mary didn't believe in,
but she certainly believed in marriage, or rather in
being married. She had no talent at all for the single
life, or even for waiting after a divorce, a break. However, once married, she made a strikingly independent
wife, an abbess within the cloister, so to speak.

In a foreword to the paperback edition of *Memories
of a Catholic Girlhood*, she speaks of the treasures gained
from her education in Catholic convent and boarding
schools, even finding a benefit in the bias of Catholic
history as taught: "To care for the quarrels of the past,
to identify oneself passionately with a cause that became, politically speaking, a losing cause with the birth

of the modern world, is to experience a kind of straining against reality, a rebellious nonconformity that, again, is rare in America, where children are instructed in the virtues of the system they live under, as though history had achieved a happy ending in American civics."

Nonconformity may be a tiresome eccentricity or arise from genuine skepticism about the arrangements of society. Think of the headache of rejecting charge cards, the universal plastic that created a commercial world in which trying to use a personal check could bring oneself under suspicion. Going along with fidelity to old-fangledness, Mary and her husband declined the cards and had to carry about large sums of money, rolls of bills, that reminded me of nothing so much as men in fedoras in gangster movies. Still they did it and I think with some amusement in a trendy restaurant or Madison Avenue shop.

So, we meet her here in 1936, marching in a Communist May Day parade, marching along with John Porter, a new man who looked like Fred MacMurray. The conjunction of romance and the events of the day is characteristic of Mary at all points in her life. At the end of her memoir two years have passed and she has covered a lot of ground: divorce, a new marriage, unhappy, that lasted seven years, "though it never recovered." Never recovered from Wilson's mistakes and shortcomings as she saw them. I would have liked Mary to live on and on, irreplaceable spirit and friend that she was; even though I must express some relief that her memoirs did not proceed to me and my life, to be looked at with her smiling precision and daunting determination on accuracy. She had her say, but I never knew anyone who gave so much pleasure to those around her. Her wit, great learning, her gardening, her blueberry pancakes, beautiful houses. None of that would be of more than passing interest if it were not that she worked as a master of the art of writing every day of her life. How it was done, I do not know.

—*Elizabeth Hardwick*
New York, December 1991

ONE

"FelLOW WORKers, join our RANKS!" It was 1936, and there I was, Mary Johnsrud, marching down lower Broadway in a May Day parade, chanting that slogan at the crowds watching on the sidewalks. "FelLOW WORKers!" Nobody, I think, joined us; they just watched. We were having fun. Beside me marched a tall fair young man, former correspondent of the Paris *Herald*, who looked like Fred MacMurray. Johnsrud was on the road with Maxwell Anderson's *Winterset*, playing his Broadway role of the blind man. I had been out of college and married to him nearly three years.

The May Day parade was, of course, a Communist thing. The American labor holiday was the first Monday in September and marked by its own parade, with union bands, which certainly did not play the "Internationale." I had watched those parades in Minneapolis with our uncle Myers. Now, as we marched, singing the "Internationale," "Bandiera Rossa" (my favorite), "Solidarity Forever," "Hold the Fort for We Are Coming" (by Hans Eisler, I thought), the marshals, mostly girls, who stepped along beside us, keeping us in line, were noticeably blond and blue-eyed, what one would today call Wasp types. That must have been Party strategy, to give the march a face-lift, in keeping with the new line, "Communism is twentieth-century Americanism." The previous year had seen the end of so-called third-period Communism and the launching of the Popular Front by Dimitrov at the Seventh Party Congress in Moscow. The point was to meet the menace of Hitler with a merging of working-class and bourgeois parties. In France last February the Popular Front (Radicals, Socialists, and Communists) had won a big victory; next month the Leon Blum government would take office and give the working class its first "congés payés." France being one of my "fields," I had followed these developments, suggestive of a René Clair film (*A Nous la Liberté*), but I was unaware of any change in the policy of the U.S. Party, even though I myself (I now see), swinging along lower Broadway, was part of it. I only observed that what people said was true: our marshals *were* very blond and blue-eyed, and the cadres of the Party, on the whole Jewish in appearance, were making themselves less visible by staying in the center of our ranks, like the filling of the sandwich. John Porter and I had been placed on the outside, where the onlookers could not fail to see us. Or hear us. Belting out "C'est la LUT-te fin-A-A-L-e," when the others were rendering " 'Tis the final conflict." Having lived and worked in Paris (he had been with Agence Havas, too), John Porter knew the words in French. And of course I chimed in with him. We were both conscious of being young and good-looking, an advertisement for the cause, and it did not bother us that the comrades had caught on to sales-manship; we were amused that the Party, in our eyes the height of innocence, could be shrewd.

Though I had been to dances organized by them at Webster Hall, the parade was my first experience of being, or looking like, a recruit. That spring and summer marked the high point of the slight attaction I felt toward Communism. I knew something about it because I had been writing book reviews for the liberal magazines *The Nation* and *The New Republic*, and Johns-rud had been acting at the Theater Union—a down-town group that was doing left-wing plays in Eva Le Gallienne's old Civic Repertory Theatre (*Peace on Earth*, *Stevedore*, *Black Pit*, *The Sailors of Cattaro*, Gorky's *The Mother;* he had been in all of them except the first two). With his Populist background, he was full of japes at the expense of the faithful among his fellow actors—Martin Wolfson, Abner Biberman, Howard Da Silva. Over his dressing-room door he had put up a sign saying "Through these portals pass some of the most beautiful tractors in the Ukraine," and on his mirror he wrote with a wax crayon "Lovestone is a Lovestoneite!" Very funny, I thought, and the comrades forgave him. As emerged a bit later, the two leading spirits of the Theater Union, Charles and Adelaide Walker, were turning into Trotskyites while John was acting there. In 1937 Adelaide's mother, Mrs. Robert Latham George, would be thanked by the Trotsky Commission for putting up members in the house she took in Mexico City during the great John Dewey hearings, but no word of that imminent crossover reached the acting company, as far as I can tell. Or maybe it did. Was that the motive behind a short-lived actors' strike—scandalous for a radical theatre, which depended on trade-union "benefits"—that Charlie Walker somehow settled?

It was at the Theater Union, at a Sunday-night benefit, that *Waiting for Lefty* was first performed. John and I were in the audience; we had an interest in how the Odets one-acter would go: a producer named Frank Merlin held an option on John's play "Anti-Climax" and also on *Awake and Sing!*, then called "I Got the Blues," which was Odets's first play. Merlin was a fat, fortyish Irishman given to deriding "ca-PIT-alism" (possibly that was how they pronounced it in Ireland); his backer, whom we called "Mrs. Nightgown," was the wife of a man named Motty Eitingon who traded in furs, with Russia. A six-month option cost $500, and neither Odets's nor John's was taken up. "Merlin's backer faded out on him," I wrote my Vassar friend Frani Blough in Pittsburgh. John's play never did get produced. Odets had better luck. He was an actor-member of the Group Theatre, which had been reluctant to do *Awake and Sing!* (Lee Strasberg did not like it), but the immense wild success of *Waiting for Lefty* downtown that night at the Theater Union— audience and actors yelling together "Strike!" "Strike!"—assured that the Group would take over *Awake and Sing!*, with Harold Clurman directing and Stella Adler as the Jewish mother ("Have a piece of fruit")—to my mind, among the few good things Odets or the Group ever did. Well. When he and John were both under option to Merlin and would meet in his office above the Little Theatre, there was some edginess between them—John with his Standard English diction, stage presence, English-style tweeds and Odets, a Party-lining Jewish boy from Philadelphia, in an old turtleneck jersey. Possibly Odets, an aspiring actor but never at home on the stage, envied John's aplomb while despising it. Or he was envious because Merlin was planning to do John's play first. It was John who thought up "Odets, where is thy sting?"—he coined it one night at our dinner table while old Clara, who ran a funeral parlor in Harlem, served smothered chicken and mashed potatoes. Afterward the witticism passed into circulation and was in Winchell or Leonard Lyons, I think.

As for Merlin, I have never found anyone who

knew where he came from or where he went to. *Variety* has no obituary notice of him in its files; though, if still alive, he would be close to a hundred. Maybe, like his Tennysonian homonym, the old necromancer is shut up somewhere in an ancient oak tree. Thinking back (to "ca-PIT-alism"), I see him as a left-wing Socialist, or even, like O'Casey, a queer kind of unorthodox Communist. Unlike Merlin, his backer, Bess Eitingon, and her husband, Motty, the importer of Russian furs, resurfaced in my life several years later, in a house in Stamford, Connecticut, but that is for another chapter. Till now, I have never put two and two together and realized that John's "Nightgowns" were they.

I had had my own class-war problems with *The New Republic*. The pipe-smoking Malcolm Cowley— "Bunny" Wilson's successor as literary editor— though a faithful fellow traveler, was too taciturn usually to show his hand. After the first time, he almost never gave me a book to review, but let me come week after week to the house on West 21st Street that was *The New Republic*'s office then—quite a ride for me on the El. Wednesday was Cowley's "day" for receiving reviewers; after a good hour spent eyeing each other in the reception room, one by one we mounted to Cowley's office, where shelves of books for review were ranged behind the desk, and there again we waited while he wriggled his eyebrows and silently puffed at his pipe as though trying to make up his mind. Sometimes, perhaps to break the monotony, he would pass me on to his young assistant, Robert Cantwell, who had a little office down the hall. Cantwell was a Communist, a real member, I guess, but unlike Cowley, he was nice. He was fair and slight, with a somewhat rabbity appearance, and he, too, came from the Pacific Northwest, which gave us something to talk about. "Cantwell tells me the story of his life," I wrote to Frani in December 1933. In 1931 he had published a novel, *Laugh and Lie Down*, and in 1934 he published a second, *The Land of Plenty*. Both were about Puget Sound and were described to me later by a Marxist critic as "Jamesian"—he counted as the only proletarian novelist with a literary style. I had not read him then; nor had I read Cowley's *Blue Juniata* or *Exile's Return* (on a theme dear to Helen Lockwood's Contemporary Press course), but with Cantwell that did not matter. After *The New Republic*, he went to work for *Time* and moved to the right, like Whittaker Chambers, who may well have been his friend. The other day someone wrote me that Lillian Hellman tried to stage a walkout from Kenneth Fearing's funeral service because Cantwell was one of the speakers. Can you imagine? Yes. Now he is dead himself. I should have liked to thank him for his interesting book *The Hidden Northwest*, which led me to Washington Irving's *Astoria*—a happy discovery. I learn from my 1978–79 *Who's Who* (he was still living then) that he was named Robert Emmett Cantwell. A misnomer, typically

Northwestern, for Robert Emmet, the Irish patriot? A spelling error by *Who's Who*? Or just no connection?

Cowley had another cohort, very different, by the name of Otis Ferguson, a real proletarian, who had been a sailor in the merchant marine. "Oat" was not in the book department; he wrote movie reviews. But he carried great weight with Cowley, though he may not have been a Marxist—he was more of a free-ranging literary bully without organizational ties. I had a queer time with him one evening when John and I went to look him up at his place on Cornelia Street, the deepest in the Village I had yet been. At our ring he came downstairs, but instead of asking us up to his place, he led us out to a bar for a drink, which seemed unfriendly, after he had given me his address and told me to drop by. I am not sure whether it was John or me who made him edgy, or the pair of us—*notre couple*, as the French say. Perhaps he and John argued about films—John had worked in Hollywood, after all. Or could it have simply been that we had come down from Beekman Place? Anyway, whatever happened that evening and whatever caused it cannot have been the reason for my sudden fall from favor at *The New Republic*. No.

It was a book: *I Went to Pit College*, by Lauren Gilfillan, a Smith girl who had spent a year working in a coal mine—one of the years when I had been at Vassar. Cowley must have thought that here at last was a book I was qualified to review, by having had the contrary experience. The book was causing a stir, and Cowley, as he handed it over to me, benignly, let me understand that he was *giving me my chance.* I sensed a reservation on his part, as though he were cautioning me not to let the book down. He was allowing me plenty of space, to do a serious review, not another three-hundred-word bit. And with my name, I dared hope, on the cover. I got the message: I was supposed to like the book. For the first time, and the last, I wrote to order. It would have been nice if I could have warmed to the task. But the best I could do was to try to see what people like Cowley saw in the book. With the result, of course, that I wrote a lifeless review, full of simulated praise. In short, a cowardly review. Rereading it now, for the first time in more than fifty years, I am amazed at how convincing I sound. In my last sentence I speak of a "terrific reality."

But then came the blow. Cowley had second thoughts about the book. Whether the Party line had changed on it or whether for some other reason, he now decided that it was overrated. I cannot remember whether he tried to get me to rewrite my review. I think he did, but, if so, he was unsatified. In any case, he printed my laudatory piece and followed it with *a correction.* The correction was signed only with initials: O.C.F. Oat, of course. In fact, it must have been he who changed Cowley's mind. As a blue-collar reader, he had looked over the Smith girl's book—or read my review of it—and responded with disgust. Which he expressed to Cowley. And, "Write that," said Cowley. Whereupon Oat did. A three-hundred-word snarl; merited or unmerited—who knows? I cannot really blame Oat for the effect of those jeers on my feelings. Cowley would hardly have told him that he had virtually *ordered* a favorable review.

But had he? Trying to be fair to him, I ask myself now whether I could have misread the signals: Could he have been telling me to pan the book? I do not think so. But either way the lack of openness was wrong. And it was a mean trick to play on a beginner; when my review came out, in May 1934, I was not yet twenty-two. I agree that a lot of the fault was mine: I should have written my real opinion, regardless of what he wanted. But abuse of power is worse than girlish weakness, and Cowley was a great abuser of power, as he proved over and over in his long "affair" with Stalinism; for this, see, in *Letters on Literature and Politics* by Edmund Wilson, edited by Elena Wilson, under "Cowley." But it cannot have been all Stalinism; he must have taken a personal dislike to me. I leave it to the reader to decide between us.

I did not write for *The New Republic* again (nor was I asked to) till six years had passed; Cowley was gone, and Wilson had returned temporarily to his old post as book editor. Meanwhile, I reviewed for *The Nation*, where kindly Joe Krutch was book editor, assisted by Margaret Marshall. For the *Herald Tribune*'s weekly "Books," Irita Van Doren, wife of Carl, told me, in her Southern voice, "We on this paper believe that there's somethin' good in evvra book that should be brought to the attention of evvra reader." No hope there for me, then, and the *Times* Sunday book review (edited by J. Donald Adams) would never let me past the secretary—their usual policy toward untried reviewers. To make some money while John was "resting," as actors say, between jobs with a series of flops and writing plays his agent could not sell, I decided to try to write a detective story, since I read so many of them. It was to be called "Rogue's Gallery," and the victim was to be based on Mannie Rousuck, but I got so interested in describing our old gallery in the French Building, with the dogs and Mannie and types like Nick Aquavella (later of the Aquavella Gallery), that I had reached the fourth chapter without managing to produce a corpse. It was a sign to me to give up.

Since October 1, 1933, John and I had been living in a one-room apartment at 2 Beekman Place, a new building opposite 1 Beekman Place, where Ailsa Mellon Bruce and Blanchette Hooker Rockefeller lived. Most months we could not pay the rent. It was a pretty apartment, painted apricot with white trim; it had casement windows and Venetian blinds (a new thing then), a kitchen with a good stove, a "breakfast alcove," and a dressing-room with bath, besides a little front hall and the main room. Good closet space. Nice elevator boys and a doorman. Fortunately, the man at Albert B. Ashforth, the building agent, had faith in John, and, fortunately also, the utilities were included in the rather high rent. The telephone company, being a "soulless corporation," unlike dear Albert B. Ashforth, kept threatening to shut the phone off, but gas and electricity would keep on being supplied to us unless and until we were evicted.

If we *were* evicted and the furniture put out on the street (which did not happen in good neighborhoods anyway), it would not be our own. We were living with Miss Sandison's sister's furniture, having not a stick to our name except a handsome card table with a cherrywood frame and legs and a blue suede top, which someone (Miss Sandison, I think it was) had given us for a wedding present. When we moved into Beekman Place, the Howlands (Lois Sandison, who taught Latin at Chapin) let us have their Hepplewhite-style chairs and the springs and mattresses of their twin beds, which we had mounted on pegs that we painted bright red and which we set up in the shape of an L, with the heads together—you couldn't have beds that looked like bedroom beds in a living-room, as our one-room was supposed to be. Instead of spreads, we had covers made of dark-brown sateen (Nathalie Swan's idea, or was it Margaret Miller's?), and at the joint of the L, where our two heads converged, we put a small square carved oak table, Lois Sandison Howland's, too, with a white Chinese crackle table lamp that we had found at Macy's.

On the walls we had Van Gogh's red-lipped "Postmaster" (John's guardian spirit) from the Hermitage and Harry Sternberg's drawing of John looking like Lenin. Then there were Elizabeth Bishop's wedding present, bought in Paris—a colored print, framed in white, rather surreal, called "Geometry," by Jean Hugo, great-grandson of the author—and Frani's wedding present—a black-framed, seventeenth-century English broadside, on "The Earl of Essex Who cut his own Throat in the Tower"—not Elizabeth's Essex, brother to Penelope Devereux, but a later one, no longer of the Devereux family. Probably the apartment had built-in bookcases, which (already!) held the 1911 *Britannica*. I am sure of that because I wrote a fanciful piece (turned down by *The New Yorker*) called "FRA to GIB." I don't know where that *Britannica*, the first of its line, came from or where it went to; maybe it was Mrs. Howland's. On the floor were, I think, two Oriental rugs, hers also, obviously. In two white *cachepots* (Macy's) we had English ivy trailing.

To reassure a reader wondering about our moral fiber and ignorant of those Depression years, I should say that Mr. and Mrs. Howland (I could never call them "Lois" and "Harold") kindly made us feel that we were doing them a service by "storing" their things while they, to economize, lived at the National Arts Club on Gramercy Park, Mr. Howland being out of a job. We had bought ourselves a tall, "modernistic" Russel Wright cocktail shaker made of aluminum with a wood top, a chromium hors d'oeuvres tray with glass dishes (using industrial materials was the idea), and six silver Old-Fashioned spoons with a simulated cherry at one end and the bottom of the spoon flat, for crushing sugar and Angostura; somewhere I still have these and people who come upon them always wonder what they are.

Late one morning, but before we had got the beds made, "Mrs. Langdon Mitchell" was announced over the house phone, and the widow of the famous (now forgotten) playwright sailed in to pay a formal call, which lasted precisely the ordained fifteen minutes, although we were in our nightclothes and she, white-haired, hatted, and gloved, sat on a Hepplewhite chair facing our tumbled sheets. We must have met this old lady at one of Mrs. Aldrich's temperance lunches in the house on Riverside Drive, where the conversation was wont to hover over "dear Sidney and Beatrice [Webb]" and Bis Meyer, my classmate, daughter of Eugene Meyer of the Federal Reserve Bank, was described as "a beautiful Eurasian," a gracious way our hostess had found of saying "Jewish." John and I had gone up to Rokeby, in the country, for Maddie Aldrich's wedding to Christopher Rand, a Yale classics major and an Emmet on his mother's side whom Maddie had met, hunting, on weekends. At the wedding, Maddie's cousin Chanler Chapman (*A Bad Boy at a Good School*, son of John Jay Chapman and model, in due course, for Saul Bellow's *Henderson the Rain King*) had spiked Mrs. Aldrich's awful grape-juice "libation" and got some of the ushers drunk. Now the couple had an all-blue apartment with a Judas peephole in the door, Chris had a job with Henry Luce, on *Fortune*, and Maddie had started a business called "Dog Walk."

Just now I spoke of dances at Webster Hall, organized by the Party. That was where, in fact, I had met John Porter (I had better start calling him "Porter," so as not to mix him up with "John"), who had been brought by Eunice Clark, the "spirit of the apples" classmate who had edited the Vassar *Miscellany News*. Eunice was always trendy, and I guess we were all what was later called "swingers"; Webster Hall was an "in" thing to do for Ivy League New Yorkers—a sort of downtown slumming; our uptown slumming was done at the Savoy Ballroom in Harlem, usually on Friday nights. Maybe real Communists steered clear of Webster Hall, just as ordinary black people did not go to the Savoy on those Friday nights when so many white people came.

I remember one Webster Hall evening—was it the Porter time?—when John and I had brought Alan Lauchheimer (Barth) with us and he found some classmates from Yale there, in particular one named Bill Mangold, who would soon be doing public relations for medical aid to the Loyalists—a Stalinist front—and with whom I would later have an affair. At Webster Hall, too, we met the very "in" couple, Tony Williams, a gentleman gentlemen's tailor (see "Dog Walk" and the Budge-Wood laundry firm), and his wife, Peggy LeBoutiller (Best's); they knew Eunice Clark and her husband, Selden Rodman, brother of Nancy Rodman, Dwight Macdonald's wife.

Selden and Alfred Bingham (son of Senator Bingham of Connecticut) were editors of *Common Sense*, a La Folletteish magazine they had started after Yale. "Alf" was married to Sylvia Knox, whose brother Sam was married to Kay McLean, from Vassar; both were trainees at Macy's. At a party at the Knoxes' I met Harold Loeb, the technocrat and former editor of *Broom*, and a character in *The Sun Also Rises* (related also to Loeb of Leopold and Loeb, murderers). Leaning back on a couch while talking to him about Technocracy and having had too much to drink, I lost my balance in the midst of a wild gesture and tipped over onto a sizzling steam radiator. Since he did not have the presence of mind to pull me up, I bear the scars on the back of my neck to this day.

Before that, Selden, in black tie, had led a walkout in support of a waiters' strike at the Waldorf, which Johnsrud and I joined, also in evening dress—Eunice was wearing a tiara. At another table Dorothy Parker and Alexander Woollcott and Heywood Broun got up to walk out, too. The Waldorf dicks chased Selden out of the Rose Room and into the basement, where they tried to beat him up. Then he was taken to be charged at the East 51st Street police station while some of us waited outside to pay his bail and take him back home to Eunice. It was all in the papers the next day, though

Johnsrud and I were too unknown to be in the story. The reader will find some of it, including Eunice's tiara and a pair of long white kid gloves, in Chapters Six and Seven of *The Group*. I always thought it was not a Communist-inspired show. Rodman and Bingham, I supposed, must have been drawn into it somehow by Heywood Broun, the labor-liberal columnist of the old *World*, who had already led a walkout on behalf of the striking waiters at the Algonquin, where he, like Dorothy Parker, regularly lunched. Yet I have just learned (fan me with a brick, please) from Harvey Klehr's *The Heyday of American Communism* that in New York, at the time, the Hotel and Restaurant Employees' Union was "dominated by two Communists, Mike Obermeier and Jay Rubin." Klehr does not mention the Waldorf strike. But in another place he writes that by 1937 (two years later) Heywood Broun was "a devoted fellow-traveler." To me, the walkout brought a different disillusionment. It was the only time I saw Dorothy Parker close up, and I was disappointed by her dumpy appearance. Today television talk shows would have prepared me.

At Selden and Eunice's apartment—in a watermelon-pink house on East 49th Street—in the course of a summer party in the little backyard, I met John Strachey, then in his Marxist phase (*The Coming Struggle for Power*) and married to Esther Murphy (Mark Cross, and sister of Gerald Murphy, the original of Dick Diver in *Tender Is the Night*). I was shocked when he went to the toilet to pee—they were serving beer—and left the door open, continuing a conversation while he unbuttoned his fly and let go with a jet of urine. English manners? I wondered. Or was it the English left?

At Dwight Macdonald's apartment near the river, on East 51st Street, I went to a cocktail party for the sharecroppers, wearing a big mustard-yellow sombrero-like felt hat from Tappé that Mannie Rousuck, a friend of Tappé's, had procured for me—as my son, Reuel, summed it up later, Mannie was "a good getter." Fred Dupee, a Yale classmate of Dwight's, was much taken with my hat; he was just back from a year in Mexico, and I was meeting him for the first time. I was struck by his very straight, almost black hair, like an Indian's, by his blue eyes, and by a certain jauntiness. This must have been about the time of his conversion to Communism. Or had that already happened in Mexico? At any rate the Party would soon put him to work on the New York waterfront, distributing leaflets; then they made him literary editor of *New Masses*. It was possibly through Fred that Dwight, who was still on *Fortune*, was giving a party for the sharecroppers and making an embarrassed speech before literally passing the hat. I was familiar with fund-raising events downtown, in the Theater Union's ambience: they charged a quarter for horrible drinks in paper cups to help the Scottsboro Boys or silicosis victims, and you sat on the floor with your legs sticking out. The Macdonald drinks were free and in glasses, and to sit on they had dark-blue outsize furniture looking like a design edict and made by a firm called Modernage.

Another Yale friend of Dwight's, Geoffrey Hellman, who wrote for *The New Yorker*, was always at those parties, which happened on a weekly basis and usually not for a cause. Every Saturday, during the party, he and Dwight would have a fight about politics (Geoffrey was a tory), and Dwight would throw him out of the apartment. During the week they would make up, until the next party, when Dwight would throw him out again. This went on as long as Dwight worked on *Fortune* and had that apartment next to Southgate on East 51st Street. When he quit, over a piece he had written on U.S. Steel that the magazine did not like, and moved downtown to East 10th Street, to a walk-up painted black like his brother-in-law Selden's, he did not have those regular cocktail parties any more or Geoffrey did not come or else a walk-up was not as good a place to throw a friend out of as a modern apartment with elevators to be rung for by an angry host; in any case, those weekly tilts stopped, though the political differences remained.

I don't think Dwight and Nancy played bridge, but Selden and Eunice did, and Johnsrud and I, if he was not acting, often played with them for small stakes, usually in their ground-floor apartment, with its Diego Rivera print and volumes of Pareto and Spengler and *The Autobiography of Lincoln Steffens*; Selden would be wearing a black shirt. If we played at our apartment on Beekman Place, we used the beautiful cherrywood card table with the blue suede top and we served Tom Collinses during the game and toasted cheese sandwiches afterward—I was suddenly learning how to cook. We played a lot of bridge during those years (when John was on the road he played poker with the stage electricians), almost always with other couples: the Rodmans, Julia and David Rumsey, Maddie and Chris Rand, maybe Rosilla (Hornblower) and Alan Breed, or our new friends, Barbara Hudnut Boston and Lyon Boston (she was Hudnut beauty products and he was an assistant district attorney). A single man, Marshall Best, who lived in our building and worked at Viking Press, was a good bridge-player and not a bad cook (his specialty was little meatballs baked in rock salt in the oven); he would make a fourth with Frani, if she was in town, or with Nathalie Swan, back from the Bauhaus and studying with Kiesler at Columbia, or my dear, droll Catholic friend Martha McGahan, who, when asked later why she supported the Loyalists, answered, "I'm a Basque."

When the bridge-playing stopped, it was a sign heralding change, though it happened so gradually that at first no one noticed. For a while, Johnsrud and I got into a fast set of poker players who played for high stakes, mostly seven-card stud, and called each other by their last names: "Mr. Lyd" and "Mrs. Lyd," for example—she had been Kay Dana, from Boston, of the class of '32, and he was Bill Lydgate, the kingpin of the new Gallup Poll. Those poker games at the Lydgates' had a funny sexual electricity about them and the sense of a power charge, maybe because most of those Wasp men in their shirt sleeves worked in the field of opinion, for Luce or George Gallup, testing it and shaping it like bread dough. After we were divorced, Johnsrud boasted to me that he had been having an affair with "Mrs. Lyd" ("Mr. Lyd" commuted to the Institute of Public Opinion Gallup had started in Princeton), and I was not surprised. She was a yellow-eyed lynxlike blonde given to stretching herself like the cats she fancied; there was always one purring on her lap or jumping from her sinuous shoulder. Like most female cat fanciers, she was a narcissist and did not care for *me*, not even bothering to call me "Mrs. John." And in fact I was out of place in that poker-faced set, all of whom, men and women, had deep, slow-spoken voices, I noticed. When it was my turn to deal, I would always declare draw, jacks or better to open, though I knew that draw, in their book, was the next thing to mah-jongg. For my part, I hated stud, five-card and seven-card alike.

After John and I were divorced, I learned that Eunice Rodman, our bridge antagonist, had been another of his sexual partners. Eunice herself told me, adding the assurance that it was me he loved—she could tell. Actually, I was unfaithful to him myself more than once, but not with anyone we saw regularly as a couple, and I feel sure he never knew. Two of my adulteries were only once, in the afternoon, and the third was with a little Communist actor who wore lifts in his shoes—too earnest for me to really like.

More important, through *Common Sense* I came to know Jim Farrell—a decisive force in my life, as it turned out. For Selden, I had written a review (very favorable) of *The Young Manhood of Studs Lonigan*, the second volume of the Studs Lonigan trilogy. Farrell called or wrote to thank me. All we had in common was being Irish, Middle Western, ex-Catholic, and liking baseball (and I was only half-Midwestern and half-Irish). But Farrell, gregarious and hospitable, took to me anyway, and when John was on the road with *Winterset*, I went to gatherings at his place, though I felt like a complete outsider. Farrell was married to or lived with an actress (Hortense Alden; I had seen her in *Grand Hotel*), but there was nobody from the theatre at those evenings. Now, half a century later, I know that she had had an affair with Clifford Odets and I wonder what Farrell made of that, which may have happened before his time.

In the apartment they shared on Lexington Avenue, the guests were all intellectuals, of a kind unfamiliar to me. I could hardly understand them as they ranted and shouted at each other. What I was witnessing was the breakup of the Party's virtual monopoly on the thought of the left. Among the writers who had been converted to Marxism by the Depression, Farrell was one of the first to free himself. The thing that was happening in that room, around the drinks table, was important and eventful. An orthodoxy was cracking, like ice floes on the Volga. But I was not in a position to grasp this, being still, so to speak, pre-Stalinist in my politics, while the intellectuals I heard debating were on the verge of post-Stalinism—a dangerous slope. Out of the shouting and the general blur, only two figures emerge: Rahv and Phillips. Farrell made a point of introducing them, and I knew who they were—the editors of *Partisan Review*. As the popular song said, my future just passed.

It was odd, actually, that I knew of the magazine; it must have had a very small circulation. But a couple who ran a stationery store on First Avenue, around the corner from our apartment, had recommended it to me, knowing that I wrote for *The Nation*. They were Party members, surely—of the type of Julius and Ethel Rosenberg, though the wife was much prettier than Ethel. And *Partisan Review* was a Party publication, the organ of the local John Reed Club. But I had no inkling of that then; skill in recognizing Communists came to me much later. When the pair of stationers showed me an early issue of the magazine, the husband running from behind the counter to fetch it, the wife proudly watching as I turned the pages, I found that it was over my head. It was devoted to an onslaught on the American Humanists—Stuart Sherman and Paul Elmer More—with a few rancorous sideswipes at the

Southern Agrarians—Allen Tate and John Crowe Ransom, the group called the Fugitives. I do not remember any fiction or poetry, only long, densely written articles in a language that might as well have been Russian. I was distantly familiar with the Humanists, having read about them in the *Bookman*, but these Agrarians were a mystery to me, and *PR*'s crushing brief against them left me bewildered. As for the dreary Humanists, I was surprised that they needed so much attacking. In fact, Rahv and Phillips and their colleagues were beating a dead horse there.

Nevertheless, to please the stationers, with whom we were friendly, I kept buying the magazine and trying my best to read it. There is a sad little sequel to my introduction to *PR*. It ceased publication when the Party cut off funds from the John Reed Clubs (it was announced that they would be replaced by an American Writers' Congress); this may have already happened when I met the editors at Farrell's. And when *Partisan Review* resumed, still edited by Rahv and Phillips but without Jack Conroy *et al.* on the masthead, it had changed color. Dwight and Fred Dupee and I and George L. K. Morris, our backer, were on the new editorial board, and *PR* was now anti-Stalinist. Some time later, maybe when my first book was published, out of the blue came a shrill letter, many times forwarded, from the Mitchell Stationers accusing me of running out on a bill John and I owed them. I cannot remember what I did about it, if anything.

In our Beekman Place apartment, besides *PR*, I was trying to read *Ulysses*. John, in the breakfast nook, was typing his play "University" (about his father and never produced), and I was writing book reviews. Every year I started *Ulysses*, but I could not get beyond the first chapter—"stately, plump Buck Mulligan"— page 47, I think it was. Then one day, long after, in a different apartment, with a different man (which?), I found myself on page 48 and never looked back. This happened with many of us: *Ulysses* gradually—but with an effect of suddenness—became accessible. It was because in the interim we had been reading diluted Joyce in writers like Faulkner and so had got used to his ways, at second remove. During the modernist crisis this was happening in all the arts: imitators and borrowers taught the "reading" of an artist at first thought to be beyond the public power of compre- hension. In the visual arts, techniques of mass reproduction—imitation on a wide scale—had the same function. Thanks to reproduction, the public got used to faces with two noses or an eye in the middle of the forehead, just as a bit earlier the "funny" colors of the Fauves stopped looking funny except to a few.

Meeting the challenge of modernism, John and I went downtown to the New School for Social Research to hear Gertrude Stein; while we were there we looked at the Orozco frescoes and compared them to Rivera. Gertrude Stein's Indian-like face and body commanded our respect, and what she said was not very difficult.

I was shocked to hear Louis Kronenberger, who wrote for *The Nation*, say angrily that she was a charlatan. "Kronenberger is a fop," declared Farrell, without pronouncing on Gertrude Stein.

John and I read Malraux's *Man's Fate*, in English, without noticing that it had a Trotskyite slant on the Chinese revolution. We read Céline (I never liked him), and one Sunday afternoon the two of us read *The Communist Manifesto* aloud—I thought it was very well written. On another Sunday we went to a debate on Freud and/or Marx—surely a Communist affair. More hazily I remember another debate, on the execution of the "White Guards" in Leningrad in 1935; this may have been a Socialist initiative, for the discussion was rancorous. Actually, that mass execution was a foreshadowing of the first Moscow trials in the summer of 1936, which ended with the execution of Zinoviev and Kamenev.

The eternal fellow traveler Corliss Lamont, son of a J. P. Morgan partner, persistently tried to seduce me when John was working or away. This pawky freckled swain sought to suborn me by invitations to dance at the new Rainbow Room, at Ben Marden's Riviera on the Palisades, and at a place in the West 50s that featured a naked girl in a bottle. But, as we danced, while I reminded him that I was married, he tried to gain his end by reasoned argument: "You wouldn't want to have just one picture, would you?" Fifty years later, he was taking my friend Elizabeth Hardwick to the Rainbow Room, still up to his old tricks. "Transitory phenomena," he said of the Moscow trials.

Besides going to the Savoy Ballroom on Friday nights, John and I had black friends, who used to come to our apartment, nervously ushered by us past the elevator boys: Nella Larsen, the novelist (*Passing*), Dorothy Peterson, the actress (she played in the Negro *Macbeth*), and her brother, who was a doctor. They were high up in the black bourgeoisie. Nella Larsen told stories that always contained the sentence "And there I was, in the fullest of full evening dress." She lived downtown, near Irving Place. The Petersons had a house in Brooklyn—we liked them, not simply because they were black, and were proud of the friendship. We also liked Governor Floyd Olson, Farmer-Labor, of Minnesota; Selden had taken us to a nightclub with him. Then he died rather young of cancer of the stomach. Probably I would have approved of his working with the Communists in his home state in 1936. In Washington, where we went with a play of John's, we saw Congressman Tom Amlie, of Wisconsin, the secretary of the bloc of Progressives in the House; he got us visitors' passes to the House and had drinks with us in our hotel room, where he told us that his committees were "Patents, Coins, and Public Buildings—that's bottoms in committees." A sad, nice man, who, unlike Olson, could not agree to working with Communist factions.

For *The Nation*, I was reviewing a number of biographies, which taught me some history—I had not taken any at Vassar. From Hilaire Belloc's life of Charles I, I learned that inflation, which entailed a shrinking of the royal revenues in terms of buying power, was the cause of the martyred king's fall. Of all the books I reviewed I was most enthusiastic about *I Claudius*; the sequel, *Claudius the God*, I liked somewhat less. Another enthusiasm was Vincent Sheean's *Personal History*, which gave me my line on Borodin and the Communist failure in China. I was greatly excited by a historical novel, *Summer Will Show*, by Sylvia Townsend Warner, which ended with the heroine sitting down in revolutionary Paris to read *The Communist Manifesto*. "Book Bites Mary," Joe Krutch quipped in a telegram on receipt of my copy from Reno. Writing that review was the closest I came to a conversion to Communism (as indeed may have been the case of the author, for whom the book seems to have been a mutant in a career whose norm was one of wild, apolitical fancifulness—*Lolly Willowes*, *Mr. Fortune's Maggot*).

As is clear from Krutch's telegram, the Warner book reversed my ordinary practice with fiction. Usually I was rough. Steinbeck's *In Dubious Battle*, Stark Young's *So Red the Rose*, *Marching, Marching* by Clara Weatherwax, *February Hill* by Victoria Lincoln—I laid about me right and left. My standards were high— higher for fiction than for biography, which could justify itself by instructiveness—as my still Latinate style seemed to attest, nay, to vaunt. I am embarrassed to recall (textually) a concluding sentence that spoke of the lack, in current fiction, "of bitter aloes and Attic salt." Oh, dear. At least I was forthright and fearless, and I was gaining a certain renown for it; I think I can say that I was truly hated by a cosy columnist in *Herald Tribune Books* who signed herself "IMP" and doted on the books I attacked.

It was this reputation, evidently, that led Charles Angoff of *The American Mercury*, a disciple of Mencken, to invite me to lunch one day. It was a business lunch; he was working as a consultant to liven up *The Nation*, and he had an idea for me: to take on the entire critical establishment in a five- or six-part series, to be called "Our Critics." Would I want to try it? Obviously I would. The state of reviewing in the United States was a scandal, far worse than today. Book-review pages, daily and Sunday, and periodicals like *The Saturday Review of Literature* (edited then by Henry Seidel Canby) were open adjuncts of the best-seller lists, book clubs, and advertisements of the publishing industry. Among the dailies and big weeklies, the one exception was the young John Chamberlain, in the daily *New York Times*, but he rarely reviewed fiction, and I doubt that he reviewed every day. Moreover, his tenure was brief.

Margaret Marshall, Joe Krutch's assistant, had come to lunch, too. We talked excitedly for a couple of hours and before we separated it was agreed that I would take on the job. Later, there were second thoughts. Freda Kirchwey, who was running the paper under Villard, decided that I was too young to be entrusted with a series of such importance; knowing what I know of her, I suppose she was afraid of me, that is, of what I might write. So a compromise was worked out: Margaret Marshall would be assigned to work on the articles with me. We would divide the research equally; then she would write half the articles, and I would write half. For instance, she would do *The New York Times Book Review*, under J. Donald Adams, while I would do *New Masses*, under Granville Hicks. There would be five articles; the first, or introductory one, we would write together. For all five articles, both our names would be on the cover.

We had fun in the New York Public Library reading-room, doing our research in back issues of magazines and newspapers and using lined cards to copy out quotations, some of them unbelievable. Peggy Marshall came from a Mormon family in Utah or Montana; she was about ten years older than I, around thirty-three, and was divorced from her husband; they had one little girl, whose custody they shared. Peggy, I soon discovered, did not have much energy; she was having an affair with a labor writer named Ben Stolberg, and both of them would lie on a sofa or daybed in her living-room, too tired to do anything, apparently too tired to go to bed and make love. Nor can I remember her ever cooking a meal.

Neither was very attractive; she was blond, grayish-eyed, and dumpy, with a sharp turned-up nose, and Stolberg was blond, blue-eyed, and fat and talked, snorting, through his nose, with a German accent. I don't know what view Stolberg took of himself, but Peggy, to my horror, saw herself as seductive. Once, when we were talking of Ben and whether he wanted to marry her, I saw her look in the mirror with a little smile and toss of her head; "Of course I know I'm kinda pretty," she said.

Not long after this, on a weekend when we were starting to do the first piece, we decided to work on it in the *Nation* office, dividing it in two. I typed my part and waited for her to do hers, so that we could turn our copy in and leave. But she could not get it written; on the sheet of paper she finally showed me, there were a few half-finished sentences. She was giggling and making a sort of whimpering sound. This was the first writer's block I had witnessed, if that is what it was. At length I took her notes and the sheet of paper from her and sat down and wrote what I thought she wanted to say. She thanked me a bit weepily, and I assured her it was O.K. I guessed that she was having a nervous breakdown, from the tension of the divorce, which was quite recent, and living with Judy, the little girl. Stolberg was probably no help.

That was how it was, for five weeks, except that soon she stopped trying and just let me write the pieces, using her notes and mine. She did manage to do half of one—the one on *The New York Times Book Review*—and made no further effort, though we talked about what would be in the articles and perhaps she suggested small changes of wording. I told Johnsrud of course but nobody else. When the pieces started coming out, the only other person to know that Peggy was not really the co-author was Freda Kirchwey. Peggy had had to tell her something to account for the fact that she was asking for more money for me, but I never knew what Freda knew exactly. They did pay me more money, and after the first week our names, at Peggy's prompting, were reversed on the cover and in the headings: my name now came first.

John did not approve of any of this. He thought I should make Peggy take her name off the whole series; he did not trust her, he said. One could not trust a woman who was as weak as that. They were buying my silence, he said. It all chimed in with things that had happened to his father when he was principal of that Minnesota high school. I said I could not demand full credit because I was sorry for Peggy. I felt sure that she had not told Freda everything. If the truth came out, when our names were already on the articles, Freda might feel she was too compromised to keep her job. That I was not getting complete credit for work I had done was less important than the fact that Peggy was on her own, with Judy, and barely able to perform. I cannot tell even now whether those were my true feelings. I was sorry for her certainly, but not *very* sorry, possibly because of that self-satisfied smile and "Of course I know I'm kinda pretty." Self-deception always chilled me. But I was the stronger, and she was the weaker, so I could not expose her. John said I would see how she repaid my generosity. I am not sure it was really generosity, but about repayment he was right, as the reader will see. She has been dead for years now; there is no reason for me to keep silent. And yet I feel guilty, like somebody repeating a slander, as I write this down.

The series on the critics was an immense succès de scandale. It was time someone did it. Peggy and I, our names now linked together for what looked like eternity, were a cynosure. Seeing her respond to the compliments that came to both of us at the parties we were invited to, I was annoyed, I found. I felt that she was *preening*. Repressing my annoyance, I behaved falsely. Between the two of us, once the series was published, no reference was ever made to the division or non-division of labor that had gone into it. Her affair with Ben Stolberg did not last very long, and somehow—I forget the circumstances—he hired me to be his secretary-typist for a book he was going to write on labor.

He was a mine of knowledge, a deviant socialist of some sort, with a witty mind (from the book he was meant to be writing: "Judge Gary never saw a blast furnace till after his death"), but he had a mammoth writer's block and a genius for wasting time when he should have been working. He had hired me on the theory that if he paid me to come every day he would have to dictate some sort of text to me. But our first week was spent buying a typewriter; under his direction I typed "Now is the time for all good men" on Remingtons and Royals and L. C. Smiths and Coronas, office models and portables, in the various typewriter stores he found in his neighborhood. I could not get him to make up his mind between them, and finally I chose one myself, and he paid for it—he had a rich woman poet as a patron. Then we spent several more days buying office supplies (choosing between weights of typewriter paper, all-black ribbons or red-and-black, sizes of manila envelopes, et cetera), till finally I was seated before a new Royal in his living-room on just the right chair, and he stood behind me.

Instead of dictating, he talked. On the awful chasm of difference between Harvard and Yale, perceptible in American intellectual history of the present day (e.g., Luce and Archie MacLeish were Yale, Franklin Roosevelt was Harvard); on the early days of John L. Lewis and the rebel mine workers of Illinois; on how I ought to go to graduate school and earn a Ph.D., even at Yale if I had to (Ben of course was Harvard), for without a Ph.D. I could never have a serious career as a critic; on old German cities in the Rhineland (Ben came from Frankfurt am Main); and on the structure of American society (America was the classless society, though not the kind Marx had pictured; Marx could not have foreseen this country of ours, where everybody, workers included, was middle-class).

I listened and laughed, my fingers idle on the keys. Some of his theories offended my patrician prejudices, for I liked to think that I came from a superior class, the professionals, who, together with a very few old-family financiers and land-poor gentry, were different from other Americans, whereas Ben scoffed and snorted at the notion of an American patriciate even more than at the notion of an American proletariat. It was easier for him to convince me of the vast distinction between Yale and Harvard, the more so as it embodied an aristocratic prejudice (Ben being, naturally, a snob in these matters, like most deep-dyed men of the left, not excepting Karl Marx). And he impressed me with the vital necessity of my having a Ph.D., to the point where I got on a train to New Haven to look at the graduate school, spending the night with Arthur Mizener, who was working on a doctorate, and his pretty wife, Rosemary Paris, the Perdita to my Leontes in the Outdoor Theatre at Vassar.

But that was the closest I got to a Ph.D. Something else had happened. When the first Moscow trial took place and Zinoviev and Kamenev were executed in August 1936 (and the Spanish Civil War began), I did not know about it, since I was in Reno. Shortly after that May Day parade, I had "told" John, who was back from playing *Winterset* on the road. I said I was in love with John Porter and wanted to marry him. This was in Central Park while we watched some ducks swimming, as described in "Cruel and Barbarous Treatment." Except for that detail, there is not much resemblance between the reality and the story I wrote two years later—the first I ever published. When I wrote that story (which became the first chapter of *The Company She Keeps*), I was trying, I think, to give some form to what had happened between John, John Porter, and me—in other words, to explain it to myself. But I do not see that I was really like the nameless heroine, and the two men are shadows, deliberately so. I know for a fact that when I wrote that piece I was feeling the effects of reading a lot of Henry James; yet today I cannot find James there either—no more than the living triangle of John, John Porter, and me.

John Porter was tall, weak, good-looking, a good dancer; his favorite writer was Remy de Gourmont, and he had an allergy to eggs in any form. He went to Williams (I still have his Psi U pin) and was the only son of elderly parents. When I met him, he had been out of work for some time and lived by collecting rents on Brooklyn and Harlem real estate for his mother. The family, de-gentrifying, occupied the last "white" house in Harlem, on East 122nd Street, and owned the beautiful old silver Communion cup from Trinity Church in Brooklyn; it must have been given to an ancestor as the last vestryman. After the Paris *Herald* and Agence Havas, Porter had worked in Sweden for the Women's International League for Peace and Freedom, but since then had been unable to connect with a job. Collecting rents on the wretched tenements still owned by his parents was his sole recourse, and most of the poor blacks who lived in them dodged him as best they could, having no earnings either. The Porters were very close with the little they had; they neither drank nor smoked and disapproved of anybody who did. The old father, who had once been an assemblyman in Albany, was deaf and inattentive, and John hid his real life from his mother.

He was in love with me or thought he was; my energy must have made an appeal to him—he probably hoped it would be catching. Despite his unemployment, dour mother, and rent-collecting, he was gay and full of charm. He was fond of making love and giving pleasure. By the time John came back from the road, Porter and I had a future planned. Together with a journalist friend who had a car, he was going to write a travel book on Mexico. Mexico was very much "in" then among sophisticated people, especially because Europe, what with Hitler and the fall of the dollar, was looking more and more forbidding. Hence John Porter and his co-author had readily found a publisher to advance $500 on a book contract with royalties.

It may be that Porter already had the idea of the Mexican book at the time he met me and merely needed the thought of marriage to spur him on. In any case, I fitted into the picture. After Reno, where my grandfather was getting me the best law firm to file for divorce, Porter would wait while I visited my grandparents in Seattle, and then the three of us would start out from New York in the friend's small car. It would be an adventure.

And Johnsrud? He took it hard, much harder than I had been prepared for. I felt bad for him; in fact I was torn. The worst was that, when it came down to it, I did not know why I was leaving him. I still had love of some sort left for him, and seeing him suffer made me know it. Out of our quarreling, we had invented an evil, spooky character called "Hohnsrud" (from a misaddressed package) who accounted for whatever went wrong. Our relations in bed, on my side, were unsatisfactory, and infidelity had shown me that with other men this was not so. It was as though something about John, our history together, made me impotent, if that can be said of women. I had no trouble even with the worn-out little actor in the Adler elevated shoes. Yet I doubt that sex was really the force that was propelling me; had we stayed together I might well have outgrown whatever the inhibition was. I was still immensely impressed by him and considered myself his inferior. Hence it stupefied me, shortly after our breakup, to hear Frani say, by way of explanation: "Well, your being so brilliant must have been difficult for him."

It is a mystery. No psychoanalyst ever offered a clue, except to tell me that I felt compelled to leave the man I loved because my parents had left *me*. Possibly. What I sensed myself was inexorability, the *moerae* at work, independently of my will, of my likes or dislikes. A sweet, light-hearted love affair, all laughter and blown kisses, like Porter himself, had turned leaden with pointless consequence. Looking back, I am sorry for poor Porter, that he had to be the instrument fated to separate me from John. And for him it *was* a doom, which took him in charge, like the young Oedipus meeting the stranger, Laius, at the crossroads. I wonder whether he may not have felt it himself as he finally set out for Mexico, where he would die of a fever after overstaying his visa and going to jail. All alone in a stable or primitive guest quarter belonging to a woman who had been keeping him and then got tired of it.

Meanwhile, though, before I left for Reno, Porter and I went out for a few days to Watermill, Long Island, where his parents still owned a moldy summer bungalow in the tall grass high up over the sea. With us was a little Communist organizer by the name of Sam Craig. I have told the story of that in the piece called "My Confession" in *On the Contrary*. The gist of it is that the Party was sending him to California in a car some sympathizer had donated. But Sam did not know how to drive. So he had asked Porter, a long-time friend, to take the car and give him driving lessons on the lonely back roads around Watermill. Sam was a slow learner, to the point of tempting us to despair for him. On the beach, all that week the red danger flags of the Coast Guard were out, and we swam only once in the rough water. In the evenings, over drinks in the moldy old house lit by oil lamps, Sam was trying to convert me to Communism. To my many criticisms of the Party, he had a single answer: I should join the Party and work from the inside to reform it. This was a variant on "boring from within," the new tactic that corresponded with the new line; the expression seems to have been first used in 1936. Evidently Sam was thinking of termite work to be done on the Party itself, rather than on some capitalist institution. Very original on his part, and he nearly convinced me.

In the end, I said I would think it over. Sam passed his driving-test and went off by himself in the car, heading west. As I wrote in "My Confession," I ask myself now whether this wasn't the old car that figured in the Hiss case—the car Alger gave to the Party. I never learned what happened to Sam, since I never saw or heard of him again. He may have perished in the desert or gone to work recruiting among the Okies or on the waterfront. And here is the eerie thing about the Porter chain of events: everyone concerned with him disappeared. First, Sam; next, the man named Weston, Porter's collaborator on the Mexican guidebook, who vanished from their hotel room in Washington after drinks one night at the National Press Club, leaving his typewriter and all his effects behind.

Porter searched for a week, enlisting police help; they canvassed the Potomac, the jails, the docks, the hospitals, they talked to those who had last seen him.

The best conclusion was that he had been shanghaied. By a Soviet vessel? Or that he had had some reason to want to disappear. But without his typewriter? A journalist does not do that. He was never found.

Meanwhile, I, too, had dropped out of the picture. I was in New York, at the Lafayette Hotel, and concurring by telephone with the decision Porter came to: to go on without Weston and get the book started, while he still had the car and half the advance. Of course I had qualms. Even though he had taken it with good grace when, on my return from Reno and Seattle, I had got cold feet about the Mexican trip. I forget what reason I gave. The fact was, I had lost my feeling for him. But I let him think I might join him once he had "prepared the way." From Washington he wrote or telephoned every day; after he left, I wrote, too, day after day, addressing my letters to Laredo, general delivery. I never heard from him again.

Late that fall, a crude-looking package from an unknown sender arrived in the little apartment I had taken on Gay Street in the Village. Having joined the Committee for the Defense of Leon Trotsky, whose members were getting a certain number of anonymous phone calls—Sidney Hook, we heard, looked under the bed every night before retiring—I was afraid to open the thing. As far as I could make out from the scrawled handwriting, it came from Laredo, on the Mexican border; conceivably there was a connection with Trotsky and his murderous enemies in Coyoacán.

I am ashamed to say that I asked Johnsrud if he would come over and be with me while I opened it. He did. First we listened, to be sure we could not hear anything ticking—but inside all we found was a quite hideous pony-skin throw lined with the cheapest, sleaziest sky-blue rayon, totally unlike Porter, who had a gift for present-giving. I had already ruled out any likelihood that the crudely wrapped package had anything to do with him, even though Laredo had been on his way. The sleazy throw confirmed this. On Johnsrud's advice probably, I wrote or wired the sender. In reply, I got a telegram: PACKAGE COMES FROM JOHN PORTER MEXICO.

That was all. At some point that autumn his mother wrote me, demanding that I pay her for the telephone calls he had made to me in Seattle. I refused. Next, his parents wanted to know, perhaps through a third party, whether I had heard from him at Christmas—they had not. But my memory here is hazy. And I cannot remember when I finally learned of his death. It was more than a year later, and it seems to me that it came to me in two different versions, from different sources. Certainly the second was from Marshall Best, the Viking Press editor who lived at 2 Beekman Place and served those meatballs baked in salt. He was a devoted friend of Porter's and, if I may say it, quite a devoted Stalinist sympathizer. By now, naturally, what with the Trotsky Defense Committee, he disliked me on political grounds. It may have given him some satisfaction to tell me a piece of news that was not only painful but also reflected poorly on me. As though I were the principal cause of Porter's death. And perhaps, in truth, I was. His mother must have thought so.

If it had not been for me, he would never have *been* in Mexico. He would still be collecting rents for his parents. And, if I had gone along with him, instead of copping out, I would *never* have let him overstay his visa, which had caused him to land in prison, which caused him to contract diphtheria or typhus or whatever it was that killed him when, on his release, the woman he had been living with let him come back and stay in her stable.

Well. As an English writer said to me, quoting Orwell, an autobiography that does not tell something bad about the author cannot be any good.

I am not sure why I lost my feeling for Porter. At the time I thought it was his letters—wet, stereotyped, sentimental—that had killed my love. The deflation was already beginning, obviously, when I met the man in the Brooks Brothers shirt on the train that was taking me west. The letters and phone calls completed the process. Whatever it was, I now realize that I positively disliked that Fred MacMurray look-alike when I saw him gazing fondly down at me when he met me on my return. The distaste was physical as well as intellectual. I could not stand him. He had become an embarrassment, having served his purpose, which I suppose was to dissolve my marriage. I was appalled, for him and for myself.

Did he notice that I had changed? Nothing was

ever said, and I tried to hide it. *"Succès?" "Succès fou!"* had been our magic formula after love-making, and *"Succès fou!"* I went on duly repeating, I imagine. I was telling myself that it was only a few days; in a few days he would have left. Such cowardice was very bad of me. If I had had the courage to tell him, he might not have started out without me. Yet I am not sure. Would my having "the heart" to tell him have made the difference? Probably the truth was that Porter *had* to go to Mexico; his bridges were burned. That applied to all three of us. Nothing could return to the *status quo ante.* John and I had left 2 Beekman Place behind, to the tender mercies of Albert B. Ashforth, who painted our pretty apricot walls another color, I suppose. The Howlands' furniture had been passed on to a friend of Alan Barth's named Lois Brown. A trunk with my letters and papers in it went to storage, never to be reclaimed. Johnsrud had moved back to the Village. While waiting for my grandfather to fix things up with Thatcher & Woodburn in Reno, I had stayed with Nathalie Swan in her parents' Georgian house in the East 80's. No, nothing could go back to what it had been. Old Clara returned to her funeral-parlor business—she was proud of having buried a fighter named Tiger Flowers. I never ate her smothered chicken again. Poor "Hohnsrud" of course had died.

Moreover, Porter was sensitive—think of his allergies. He must have heard the difference on the telephone while I was still in Seattle; I am a fairly transparent person. And if he guessed my changed feelings, he kept it strictly to himself. The question I should ask myself is not did he know, but how *soon* did he know. It is a rather shaking thought.

TWO

The one-room apartment I moved into on Gay Street had eleven sides. I counted one day when I was sick in bed. The normal quota, including floor and ceiling, would have been six. But my little place had many jogs, many irregularities. There was a tiny kitchen and a bath suited to a bird. It had been furnished by the owner of the building, an architect by the name of Edmond Martin whose office was on Christopher Street. I am not sure he ever built anything, but he had a genius for getting the good out of space that was already there. At no extra charge, he made me a thin, teetery bookcase to fit into one of the nine perpendiculars—he loved to be given a problem. One nice feature was that the little bath had a window beside it so that you could look at the sky while you bathed. Another amusing oddity of the apartment was that, small as it was, it had two street entrances: one on Gay Street and one, leading through a passageway, to Christopher Street, where the bells and mailboxes were. Mr. Martin, who was an engaging person, owned another old house, on Charles Street, in which Elizabeth Bishop lived. Her living-room was bigger than mine and had a fireplace, I think. It must have been through her that I found the Gay Street apartment after Porter left. Or else it was the other way around and she found her place through me. All Mr. Martin's rents were reasonable, and he took good care of his properties.

My bed was a narrow studio-couch with a heavy navy-blue cover and side cushions, which made the room into a living-room, and I had a desk with drawers beside a recessed window. I could entertain only one couple at a time for dinner by putting two chairs at a card table and sitting on the studio-bed myself. I invited Farrell and Hortense (Farrell, a true-blue Irishman, always asked for more mashed potatoes), Chris and Maddie Rand, and I cannot remember who else. Probably Martha McGahan and Frani, together or separately. Margaret Marshall.

All this was very different from our life on Beekman Place; it was as though the number of my friends had shrunk to fit the space I now lived in. Not counting Johnsrud, who came around from time to time and made biting remarks, the only men I knew were Mr.

Martin and the husbands of friends. The assiduous men who had been after me while I was married, such as Corliss Lamont and the absurd Lazslo Kormendi, had vanished. Nobody took me out to dinner, and when I did not cook something for myself, I ate at a second-floor restaurant called Shima's on Eighth Street, where the food was cheap and fairly good. But it typed you to be a regular at Shima's, because no one, male or female, ever went there with a date. Today it would be called a singles' restaurant, with the difference that there were no pick-ups. Night after night at dinnertime, I faced the choice of hiding my shame at home or exposing it at Shima's. I always took a book to bury myself in, on the ostrich principle.

Sometimes on Sundays, Farrell's kindly publisher, Jim Henle of Vanguard Press, asked me to lunch at the house he and his wife, Marjorie, had in Hartsdale, half an hour or so from New York. But I could not hope to meet any unattached men there, I discovered. It was an office group like a family, headed by Evelyn Schrifte, eventually Henle's successor at Vanguard; the only author present was Farrell. Still, going out there was fun; I liked the Henles. But apart from those Sundays, the only break in the monotony of my first months as a divorcee on Gay Street was when the man in the Brooks Brothers shirt—real name George Black—came from Pittsburgh and took me to the World Series. The Giants were playing the Yankees, and Fat Freddie Fitzsimmons was pitching in the game we went to. When, at his insistence, I brought the "man" home, so that he could see how I lived, he was shocked and begged me to move. He still thought he wanted me to marry him, even though I would no longer let him make love to me. In the story I wrote about it nearly four years later (on the Cape during the fall of France), the heroine sees him several times in New York posthumously to their love-affair on the train, but I remember only the once—the excitement of being at the World Series (and with a National League fan; he had arranged our box-seat tickets through the Pittsburgh Pirates), and having dinner with him afterward—at Longchamps, it must have been. I have a very faint recollection of a duck he had shot that started to smell in my icebox because I did not know how to take off the feathers and cook it. In the story, I changed several things about him, including where he was from, in case his wife might somehow come upon it and recognize him. Really he lived in Sewickley, a fashionable outskirt of Pittsburgh, belonged to the Duquesne Club, and worked for American Radiator and Standard Sanitary—plumbing. The man in the story was in steel. (When it came out in 1941 in *Partisan Review*, Jay Laughlin of New Directions was telling people that the "man" was Wendell Willkie, who had run for president the year before.) George Black's ardor was an embarrassment to me— a deserved punishment. Hard up as I was for male company, I kept him out of sight. None of my friends knew about him, and until now I have not told his name.

Those must have been the harshest months of my life. My grandfather was sending me an allowance of $25 a week, since the Capital Elevator stocks I had inherited from the McCarthys were not paying dividends any more, or very little. I did some reviews for *The Nation* and I looked for a job. Someone sent me to a man who lived in the St. Moritz Hotel and needed a collaborator for a book he was writing on the influence of sunspots on the stock market. No. At last Mannie Rousuck, now with Ehrich Newhouse and starting on his upward climb, was able to give me half a day's work at the gallery, writing descriptions of paintings for letters he sent to prospects. Some of the addressees were the same ones we had written to at the Carleton Gallery—Ambrose Clark, Mrs. Hartley Dodge—though my subjects were no longer just dogs but English sporting scenes with emphasis on horses, English portraits, conversation pieces, coaching scenes. I think he paid me $15 a week, which, with the allowance from my grandfather, was more than enough to support me. I could even serve drinks.

Nonetheless I was despondent. If I had been given to self-pity, I would surely have fallen into it. I did not much regret breaking up with John, especially because he was taking a sardonic, mock-courteous tone with me, and I had almost forgotten Porter. It was not that I wanted either of them back. I saw plenty of John

as it was, and I would have been horrified if Porter had appeared on my doorstep. There was no room for him in my multi-faceted apartment. My renting it showed that I had not thought of him as being in my life at all.

At some time during the autumn I had driven to Vermont with Mannie, to see a collection of sporting art that would be very important to him and, incidentally, to see the autumn leaves. On another Saturday I had gone up to Vassar to see Miss Sandison (Miss Kitchel was on sabbatical), and we had talked of my discovery of left-wing politics, which she knew all about, as it turned out, having subscribed to *New Masses* or read it in the library while I was still in college. Then we talked of love, which she knew about, too, even more to my surprise. I can still hear her light, precise voice tell me that you must "learn to live without love if you want to live *with* it." In other words, not to depend on having love. You must come to real love free of any neediness. This thought greatly struck me, and still does. I am sure it is true but, unlike Miss Sandison, I am not up to it. I have seldom been capable of living without love, not for more than a month or so. That afternoon, in her small sitting-room in Williams, where our Renaissance seminar had been held, pouring tea again, she told me a little about her private life. There had been a man (at Yale, I gathered), but, though they were lovers, they did not marry. "I could think *rings* around him," she remembered with a mournful little laugh. Maybe that was always the fly in the ointment. She was too intelligent for the men she chanced to meet.

I was moved by that long conversation, inspired by it to try to be like Miss Sandison. She was clear-eyed, a heroine like Rosalind and Celia. I was not so brave. Many years later, after her retirement, her dauntless character was put to the test. First of all, on becoming an *emerita*, she worked as a volunteer for the Civil Liberties Union in New York (single-handed, she said in a shocked tone, she had straightened out the awful disorder of their files), and also for the Heart Association, that perhaps in memory of Miss Kitchel, with her flushed cheeks, who had died in Toledo of heart trouble. In New York, after a while, Miss Sandison lived alone; her sister had died, too. But then she had to give up her volunteer work, because she was going blind. Frani, who lived nearby, used to go in and read to her and wrote to me in Paris about it. I intended to write, so that Frani could read the letter to her. But I didn't. Time passed. Her address, in Frani's handwriting, pleaded with me daily on my desk. At last I learned from Frani that it was too late: Miss Sandison was dead. She had found she was going deaf, on top of being blind, and took the logical step. Without telling anyone, she carefully arranged her suicide—death-by-drowning—putting weights in the pockets of her dress, filling the bathtub, and climbing in. Perhaps she took some sleeping pills, to keep herself from involuntarily coming up again. She even put a message for the cleaning-woman on her door, so that the woman would not be frightened by finding her body. I do not know how she managed, with only the sense of touch to help her. But she did.

And to think that I never wrote. Of course that September or October day was not the last time I saw her. We were reunited a number of times—with Miss Kitchel when I was teaching at Bard forty minutes off up the Hudson—and then alone. I remember things she said during those later meetings, especially the first one, when I had left Wilson and was living with Reuel, aged seven, in Upper Red Hook, though then it was Miss Kitchel who spoke the immortal sentence over our Old Fashioneds: "Tell us you didn't marry him for love!" She was speaking, naturally, for them both. I remember how well they both looked, Miss Kitchel with her slightly faded blue eyes and Miss Sandison with her deep, sparkling dark ones, and the Covermark now hiding the disfiguring birthmark on her cheek. I was filled with love for both of them, and the fact that I was teaching literature—my maiden effort—put us on terms of greater parity. Yet, of all our meetings, the most memorable for me has always been that fall afternoon in 1936 with Miss Sandison when I was trying to learn from her how to live alone. In reality I was doing it at Bard in those first months of teaching; I had firmly given up any notion of a new marriage and pictured myself romantically as a sort of secular nun. But Miss Sandison and Miss Kitchel never came to see me at Bard—now, I wonder why not; perhaps just the fact that they were not motorized and I was. Miss Sandison never saw my place on Gay Street or any place I lived, even when it was with her sister's furniture. I always went to her, at Vassar, and if I took her and Miss Kitchel out, it was downtown to a Pough-keepsie restaurant. This points to a reticence in our relation, characteristic of Miss Sandison, though not of me. She had read Wilson's work and she and Miss Kitchel had listened to Johnsrud read his first play aloud on their screened back porch. But she probably knew very little, unless from other sources, of John Porter and his successors in my life.

We talked that day about Granville Hicks and *New Masses*, Marxian criticism, so called then (now it is "Marxist"). I wanted to impress Miss Sandison with the fact that I had become political ("radicalized" was the word in the sixties), yet, finding that she, too, was perfectly abreast of the new tendencies, I was able to open my heart to her and suggest the doubts I felt. These were *literary* doubts, I emphasized; I had no disagreement with the political side of the magazine. But in the literary pages there was a smell of Puritan-ism. I was reminded of the Marprelate Controversy that we had read about in her senior seminar on the English Renaissance—the same fanatic spirit. Not just "Granny" Hicks, but a lot of those *New Masses* re-viewers brought to mind a character in Ben Jonson's

Bartholomew Fair, the hateful Puritan militant wonderfully named Zeal-of-the-Land-Busy. In the Marprelate quarrel, I had been rather on the side of the Established Church, whose pamphleteers had been university wits. But above all I had responded to the noble, balanced periods of Richard Hooker (*Ecclesiastical Polity*), the great defender of the episcopate and anticipator of Locke—Miss Sandison had inspired me to read him.

It came to me that afternoon that the Elizabethans, her "field," still constituted for me a sort of wondrous paradigm, a model in which the inflections or "cases" of literary practice were perennially recognizable. Spenser's friend the pedant Gabriel Harvey, for instance, could have been a perfect *New Masses* contributor and advocate of the prolet-cult in literature. Harvey, the son of a ropemaker in the Norfolk town of Saffron Walden, was a species of crypto-puritan, possessed by a baleful hatred of the University Wits; he attacked the dying Robert Greene and was wonderfully counterattacked by Thomas Nashe. As a Latinist, he wanted to introduce the meters of classical verse into English poetry—in other words, to imprison it in a strait-jacket. I think the pedant and the puritan can never be far apart. To this day, the uncouth Harvey, for me, stands at the antipodes of true talent and its correlate, freedom, and I do not forgive Edmund Spenser, defender of the cruel Irish repression, for being his friend. Have with you to Saffron Walden, I say with Nashe.

Miss Sandison, of course, was pleased to see that the lessons of her seminar had not been lost on a favorite pupil. She was a friend of freedom herself— why else did she go to work for the ACLU? So I wonder how she took the fact that I was still leaning toward Stalinism. As I say, it was their *literary* practices that I found offensive. I had actually been talking of voting for Browder in the November election, casting what would be my first vote. Had I changed my mind? It depends on the date. Did I go up to Vassar before or after I woke up and found myself on the Trotsky Committee? Almost certainly before, since that took place in November. I have told the story in "My Confession," and the point I made there was that it happened by pure chance. At a cocktail party for Art Young, the *New Masses* cartoonist, Jim Farrell, who seemed to be taking some sort of canvass, asked me if I thought Trotsky was entitled to a hearing, and naturally I answered yes, without any clear idea of what he was being charged with. Having been in Reno and Seattle, I had missed the news stories of the first Moscow trials. And I do not know how it was that I had been invited to what was presumably a Stalinist party, still less why Farrell had. Apparently the lines were not yet clearly drawn. But once I answered yes (and Farrell, it seemed, wrote my name down), my goose was cooked. A few mornings later, opening my mail, I found my name on a letterhead; it was a group that was demanding Trotsky's right to a hearing, and also his "right to asylum." I was angry that my name had been used without my consent, but before I had time to register my protest by withdrawing it, my telephone began ringing: Stalinist acquaintances urging me to *take my name off that committee*. Other signers, like Freda Kirchwey, as I learned from the day's paper, were promptly capitulating to the application of pressure. This only hardened my resolve, as anybody who knew me could have guessed. I let my name stay—a pivotal decision, perhaps *the* pivotal decision of my life. Yet I had no sense of making a choice; it was as if the choice had been thrust on me by those idiot Stalinists calling my number. I did not feel I was being brave; on the other hand, the Freda Kirchweys hurrying to withdraw their names looked to me like cowards. Though I was unconscious of having come to a turning point, the great divide, politically, of our time, I did know that I had better find out something about the cause I had inadvertently signed up with. Minimally I had to learn the arguments for Trotsky's side.

Luckily I was the daughter and granddaughter of lawyers. And even more luckily a pamphlet had been issued analyzing the evidence in the first trial from "our" point of view, that is, on the assumption that, despite the defendants' confessions, Trotsky was innocent of having conspired with the Nazis to overthrow the Soviet state. To my relief, the pamphlet was extremely convincing. I read it with care, testing the arguments as though I were preparing for an exam.

And they held water. Yet I cannot remember who wrote it. I think there was a sequel dealing with the second trial, of Pyatakov and Radek, which took place in January. I remember poring over the verbatim reports of both trials on my studio-couch in Gay Street. Yet I have no recollection of when or how the Trotsky Committee was formed. I know that there was already a committee and I was on it by February 14, 1937, because I remember the meeting that night in Farrell's apartment and that I was the only one who noticed that it was St. Valentine's Day, which I guess said something about all concerned.

In recent years I have read more than once that Edmund Wilson was on the Trotsky Committee. What an opportunity for us to have got to know each other! But I never saw him at any Committee meeting.

Being on the Committee marked the end of my awful solitude. Some time around Christmas things began to improve. I was meeting people—*men*. Part of that had to do with the Committee ("Dear Abby" in her column advises her lonely-heart readers to join a group—church group, she recommends), but a lot was coincidence. For instance, Bob Misch of the Wine and Food Society. How had I met him? Maybe through my friends Gene and Florine Katz. Misch was in the advertising business, single, German Jewish, and the very active secretary of the wine and food organization, whose head was André Simon, in London. He fancied himself as a cook and a knowledgeable bon vivant.

His short, stocky, dark, well-fed body made me think of a pouter pigeon. Probably someone took me to one of his Wine and Food tastings: on a series of tables various wines were grouped around a theme—Rhine wines, Loire wines, Burgundies—one sampled them, made notes, and compared. On the tables there were also little things to eat, "to clear the palate," and probably water to rinse your mouth out. It was educational, it was intoxicating, and it was free. After the first time, my name was on their list, and I always accepted. Soon he was asking me to the little dinners he gave in his West Side apartment, quite evidently as his partner; his specialty was black bean soup with sherry and slices of hard-boiled egg. The reader will find something like those dinners in the chapter called "The Genial Host" in *The Company She Keeps*. If I may give an opinion, it is the weakest thing in the book. No doubt that is because I was unwilling to face the full reality of the relationship. In real life I slept with him and in the story I don't. I suppose I was ashamed. Misch was eager to make me expensive presents (such as handbags) and to do services for me that I didn't want. Even after I stopped sleeping with him, which was soon, he kept on asking me to those dinners, and I kept on accepting, because of his insistence and because, as the chapter says (though without mentioning sex between us), I was not quite ready to break with him, being still "so poor, so loverless, so lonely."

The guests at those little dinners were mostly Stalinists, which was what smart, successful people in that New York world were. And they were mostly Jewish; as was often pointed out to me, with gentle amusement, I was the only non-Jewish person in the room. It was at Misch's that I first met Lillian Hellman, who had been brought, I guess, by his friend Louis Kronenberger. But I may mix her up with another Stalinist, by the name of Leane Zugsmith. It was with Hellman, just back from Spain, that I had angry words about the Spanish Civil War. Probably, as happens in the chapter, I grew heated about the murdered POUM leader, Andrés Nin.

That same evening (more or less as related), I started on a brief affair with Leo Huberman (*Man's Worldly Goods*), who was a suave sort of Stalinist and married. But I no longer needed Misch's dinners to meet new people, not even new Stalinists. Suddenly the woods were full of them. If I met Huberman there, I was also seeing Bill Mangold (not Jewish; it means a kind of beet in German), a Yale classmate of Alan Barth's whom I had first met at Webster Hall a couple of years before. Now he took me to dinner, at a fun place where we danced. He was separated from his wife; he was going to a psychoanalyst (the first analysand in my personal history); he was amusing and worked for medical aid to the Loyalists in Spain, a Stalinist front. We did not discuss politics, which no doubt eased the difficulty of having a quite active and friendly love-affair with a distinctly Trotskyist girl. Of all the men I slept with in my studio-bed on Gay Street (and there were a lot; I stopped counting), I liked Bill Mangold the best. Until I began to see Philip Rahv.

Once I got started, I saw all sorts of men that winter. Often one led to another. Most of them I slept with at least one time. There was Harold ("Hecky") Rome, who wrote the lyrics for the ILGWU musical *Pins and Needles* ("Sing me a song with social significance"); we cooked a steak together one night in his apartment—perfect. There was a little man who made puppets that appeared on the cover of *Esquire* and another little man, very droll and witty, who was married and worked for a publisher—he came to my place from the office in the afternoon and was a bit nervous despite his aplomb. There was a truck driver whose name I have forgotten, if I ever knew it, whom I met in the bar at Chumley's. I did not go to bars alone, so someone must have taken me—probably John—and then left.

It was getting rather alarming. I realized one day that in twenty-four hours I had slept with three different men. And one morning I was in bed with somebody while over his head I talked on the telephone with somebody else. Though slightly scared by what things were coming to, I did not *feel* promiscuous. Maybe no one does. And maybe more girls sleep with more men than you would ever think to look at them.

I was able to compare the sexual equipment of the various men I made love with, and there were amazing differences, in both length and massiveness. One handsome married man, who used to arrive with two Danishes from a very good bakery, had a penis about the size and shape of a lead pencil; he shall remain nameless. In my experience, there was usually a relation to height, as Philip Rahv and Bill Mangold, both tall men, bore out. There may be dwarfish men with monstrously large organs, but I have never known one. It was not till later, after my second divorce, that I met an impotent man or a pervert (two of the latter). Certainly sexual happiness—luxurious contentment—did make quite a difference in my feeling for a lover. Yet it was not always the decisive factor. None of my partners, the reader will be relieved to hear, had a venereal disease.

The best news was that I had found a job in publishing. Before I went to Reno, Eunice Clark, no longer married to Selden, had taken me to the cafeteria in the Central Park Zoo (really a menagerie), where at some outdoor tables near the seal pool a group of young people of the intellectual sort gathered in the late afternoon to drink beer and watch the seals. There I had met Pat Covici, of the firm Covici-Friede, who was aware of my *Nation* articles. I told him I was looking for a job in publishing. One day in the fall, when I was long back from Reno, there was Mr. Covici again, white-haired and benevolent, who claimed to have been looking for me. "You are as evanescent as a cloud," he told me, in his accented voice, and offered me a job in his office.

At Covici, I read manuscripts and looked for new

authors in quarterly magazines like the *Southern Review*: when I came on a story I liked, I would write the author and ask for a possible sample of a longer work. One of those I wrote to was Eudora Welty. Besides this scouting and manuscript-reading, I edited, proofread, and farmed out texts in foreign languages to qualified readers to report on. Opposite me, in a medium-sized office, sat a long-nosed Stalinist woman named Miss Broene, who intensely disapproved of my politics, my many telephone calls and long lunch hours, my arrival time at work in the morning. Our boss was Harold Strauss (later at Knopf), who had a lisping disapproval of what he called "photographic realism," meaning specifically my friend Jim Farrell. Strauss was not especially political, but there were several Stalinists in our top management, not including Mr. Covici, thank God. Mr. Covici read literary books and magazines and was a fatherly sort of person. One day he took me to lunch with his star author, John Steinbeck, at the Prince George Hotel. I did not care for Steinbeck's work (as I had said in *The Nation*) and I did not care for him. He reciprocated.

I am eternally grateful for having learned the mechanics of publishing at Covici, how to copy-edit and how to proofread. I learned printer's signs and the marks to make on a manuscript before sending it to the printer. For instance, you lower-cased a capital letter by drawing a slash through it; to upper-case, you drew three lines under a letter and wrote "cap" in the margin; if you wanted to retain a hyphen, you made it into an "equals" sign. In all this, the dour Miss Broene, who had turned Communist after being fired from Consumer Research for union organizing, was instructive and really quite helpful, all the while she was denouncing me to the office chapter of the Book and Magazine Guild for my persistent lateness to work.

Also to enter on the plus side was Philip Rahv. Remembering him from Farrell's parties, I called him one day when we needed a reader for a German text Mr. Covici was considering. Or it may have been the memoirs in Russian of the wonderful Angelica Balabanov, who had been close to Mussolini in his socialist days, then close to Lenin, and was now a left-wing anti-Communist. Rahv, who had been born in the Ukraine of Zionist parents, knew Russian, German, and Hebrew and he was able to read some French. When I called him, he came to the Covici office, and we talked a little in the waiting-room. He had a shy, soft voice (when he was not shouting), big, dark lustrous eyes, which he rolled with great expression, and the look of a bambino in an Italian sacred painting. I liked him. Soon he was taking me out to dinner in the Village, holding my elbow as we walked, and soon we were lovers. I gave up Bill Mangold with a small pang. Politically Rahv and I were more alike—he was breaking at last with the Party and joining the Trotsky Committee—and I was greatly excited by his powerful intellect, but Mangold, with his Yale background, was more my kind of person. Had I not got to know Rahv, I might have married Mangold, if he ever got his divorce. Years later an avatar of him took form in *The Group*, in the figure of Gus Leroy, the publisher, with whom Polly Andrews, poor girl, is in love.

Rahv worked on the Writers' Project—part of President Roosevelt's WPA program—and did occasional reviews for *The Nation*. But he had no other source of income, except odd jobs like the one he was doing for Covici. That did not trouble me. It only meant that we couldn't get married. Somewhere there was a wife named Naomi, whom I never saw. He had lived apart from her for a long time but could not pay for a divorce. But we did not think of marriage anyway. I believed in free unions, and so, I guess, did he. He and William Phillips dreamed of reviving *Partisan Review*, but for that they would have had to have money or an organizational tie, such as the one with the Party that they had lost when they crossed over. When we first became lovers, Philip, as I recall, had not yet met Dwight Macdonald, who in turn would introduce him to his Yale friend George L. K. Morris (of the Gouverneur Morris family; his brother was Newbold), an American abstract painter and our future backer.

I believe I had been instrumental in the de-Stalinization of Dwight. When he left *Fortune*, over their censoring of his U.S. Steel article, I took him downtown to lunch with Margaret Marshall, so that he could have an outlet for his views in *The Nation*'s back pages.

In the course of one of those lunches I discovered that dear Dwight actually believed in the Moscow trials. Once he was set straight by the two of us, he swiftly rebounded as far as one could go in the opposite direction; characteristically, he did not come to rest at a mid-point, such as entering the Socialist Party. Almost before I knew it, he was an embattled Trotskyite, of the Schachtmanite tendency. Meanwhile, through me or through Fred Dupee, he met Rahv and Phillips, who were already seriously talking to Fred with a view to his leaving *New Masses* to join them in a revived, anti-Stalinist *PR* and take a list of their subscribers with him. Dwight brought George Morris into the project, proposing to make him the art critic, with a monthly column, and the new *PR* was born.

By early summer, while all this was starting to happen, Philip and I had moved in together. The Gay Street apartment was too small for us (Philip, though still slender then, was a big man), but by good luck I had friends, Abbie Bregman and his wife, Kit, a descendant of Julius Rosenwald—Sears, Roebuck—who had a Beckman Place walk-up apartment that was going to be empty all summer. Unless I wanted to use it? Of course I accepted; the problem was how to convey that there would be another occupant, to them a complete stranger. Well, I told them, and they still urged me to use the place and the maid who came with it. Thus Philip and I found ourselves living amid severely elegant modern furnishings, all glass, steel, and chrome on thick beige rugs. I think Philip felt compromised by that apartment (which did not resemble either of us) and by the Sears, Roebuck money behind it, which did not resemble us either. He was embarrassed to receive his friends, such as Lionel Abel, whom I remember there one night as a malicious, watchful presence out of Roman comedy.

That was perhaps why we quarreled so much that summer, although we were greatly in love. It was a class war we fought, or so he defined it. I defended my antecedents, and he his. He boasted of Jewish superiority in every field of endeavor, drawing up crushing lists of Jewish musicians and scientists and thinkers—Einstein, Marx, Spinoza, Heine, Horowitz, Heifetz—with which no Gentile list could compare. He invited me to look at the difference between Marx and Engels. I could only argue that in literature and the visual arts Jews did not excel: *we* had Shakespeare and Michelangelo, the Russians, Flaubert. . . . Philip retorted that literature and the visual arts were mindless in contrast to mathematics and music. And what about Proust and Kafka? His forceful assertions, punctuated by short, harsh laughs, were arousing anti-Semitic feelings in me, which, to my shame, were put into words. Scratch a Gentile and you find an anti-Semite was his reply.

He was a partisan of what he called "plebeian" values—he loved that word. I stuck up for patrician values, incarnate, as I imagined, in the professional class I issued from, exemplified by my grandfather. Lawyers were the hirelings of the bourgeoisie, he rebutted—petty-bourgeois parasites. I did not even belong to the big-bourgeois class. That was the cruelest thrust. As for the other side of my family, it delighted him to say that the Irish were the bribed tools of imperialism—he had found the phrase in Marx. I always wondered what it applied to. Marx could hardly have been thinking of Irish cops—New York's finest. In the England of his day, there were no Irish bobbies. But whether or not Marx said it, the phrase amused me and has stuck in my mind.

Anyway we argued amid the glass and the chromium. Philip brought an enormous zest to the exercise. Dispute was his art form. In some part of his quite complex mind, it entertained him to hear us go at it. For example: Trotsky maintained that you could not build socialism in one country. "In one country!" Philip would comment, listening to us. "Why, you can't build socialism in one apartment!" That did seem to be so. We polarized each other. He could always offend me by declaring that I was bourgeois because I could not learn to think like a Marxist. I was far from being bourgeois, compared with the genuine article, but I do have a bourgeois side, which comes out in my love of possessions, cooking, gardening. Yet aren't those peasant traits, too?

During that summer the maid who came with the apartment must have stolen my mother's diamond la-

valliere and other odd bits of jewelry—my sole remaining links with my "bourgeois" or, as I thought,
patrician past. I do not see who else could have taken
them, since nobody else had access to the apartment
and I never locked anything up. I was sorry for the
loss, so irreparable, and because thieving is vile. But
that was the price I paid for the loan of a Beekman
Place apartment. Maybe the woman had reasoned that
Philip and I were "robbing" the Bregmans by living
in their apartment rent-free.

To earn a little more money, I worked that summer
with a collaborator on a book called *Kaltenborn Edits
the News*, a collection of writings and radio broadcasts
by the well-known commentator H. V. Kaltenborn. It
was really a ghost-writing job, because Mr. Kaltenborn
had sold the publisher a stack of manuscript that
proved to be mainly carbons—not just in duplicate,
but in triplicate—of old, unusable broadcasts. Possibly
he had done so in good faith; he had just never looked
at the mass of copy he turned in. Faced with the fact,
my collaborator and I wrote a new book for him,
dividing the material into chapters according to our
tastes: I did France, Spain, and the U.S. automobile
industry; my co-worker, a *New York Times* writer, did
England, Germany, and a wonderfully named chapter
about the Balkans, "Little Firebrands." We met once
a week in Mr. Kaltenborn's pleasant garden in Brooklyn Heights, drank spritzers with Mr. and Mrs. Kaltenborn (a charming German woman), and reviewed

our work to date. I doubt that Mr. Kaltenborn ever read the entire text—an amalgam of *New York Times* middle-of-the-road politics, my Trotskyizing, and the deep conservatism of his original broadcasts, bits of which we used as filler. Then, toward the middle of the summer, his son turned up from Harvard and actually read a good part of the book his father would be signing. The young man, a Stalinist and a fairly bright boy, was horrified—especially, I guess, by my contributions—and tried to undo the damage by re-writing parts himself. In the end, probably not even the publisher, still another Stalinist, read the whole book through. But it came out, this all-around rip-off, and I own a copy of it that Arthur Schlesinger bought me as a present in a second-hand bookstore in Cambridge. Since only Mr. Kaltenborn was on a royalty basis, I have no idea how the sales had been.

Philip had no interest in my work on the Kaltenborn book; I am not sure that he ever met my collaborator. He and the others were busy lining up articles for the new *PR*. During the hot weather we went out sometimes to a little house Dwight and Nancy were renting at Brookfield Center, in Connecticut, where there was a natural pool made by a pot-hole in a stream. We all swam naked there and argued about Henry James. Philip's long love-affair with James had begun; at Vassar I hadn't cared for him—neither had Miss Kitchel and Miss Sandison. Fred Dupee was a natural Jamesian; I no longer remember where Dwight stood. One Sunday morning on the breakfast table I typed out a devastating review for *The Nation* of Frederick Prokosch's *Seven Who Fled*, which the others read and approved. Despite our failure to "build socialism in one apartment," it was a happy time. We looked fondly on each other. I read *The Eighteenth Brumaire of Louis Bonaparte* and liked it. He liked Frani and Nathalie and Martha McGahan, who despite being a Catholic supported the Loyalists, saying "I'm a Basque" with her dark twinkle. Johnsrud came once to Beekman Place to have drinks or dinner with us and was not very friendly.

We followed with passion and anger the fortunes of the war in Spain; before it was over, I knew more about the Ebro than I ever knew about the Battle of the Bulge. On account of the Japanese invasion of Manchuria, I was boycotting silk, buying cotton-mesh stockings at Wanamaker's, which in those days was a downtown department store near Astor Place. I was smoking cigarettes with the union label—Raleighs, I think they were—though I liked Luckies better. Philip was less committed to consumer boycotts, suspecting, I guess, that they were bourgeois.

The Second Congress of the League of American Writers occurred early in June, before we moved into the Bregmans' apartment. This was a pure Stalinist front. With a certain temerity our small group of Trotsky defenders, all writers, elected to take part, to disrupt the proceedings if we could. William Phillips's account in his memoir, *A Partisan View*, is quite different from my memory of the event. He says that he and Philip did not want to go (to the panel on literary criticism) but that Dwight and I insisted. I don't remember any disagreement among us. At the meeting I chiefly recall one orator declaring, in evident reference to us, that there were some who "looked for pimples on the great smiling face of the Soviet Union"—those pimples were the Moscow trials. And I remember Philip's saying to me of another orator that he "waved the bloody shirt"—an expression I had never heard before and did not understand. It may have been that day that I first saw Martha Gellhorn —blond and pretty, talking about Spain. Or was it Martha Dodd, daughter of our former ambassador to Germany? Either one could have served as a marshal in the previous year's May Day parade. That night, at a vast meeting in Carnegie Hall, Hemingway spoke and Donald Ogden Stewart, to a tumult of applause. We all went and sat in the gallery but did not try to heckle; we would have been *too* unpopular. On another night, I went to a *Nation*-sponsored appearance by André Malraux, who spoke for Spain at Mecca Temple; I noticed the trembling of his hands. In Spain he had been converted to Stalinism, and I thought it was sad.

I remember a downtown meeting of some Trotskyist group where I first saw Diana Trilling; with her dark eyes and flaring nostrils, she looked like Katharine Cornell. Among Stalinist males, I heard, the Trotsky-

ists were believed to have a monopoly of "all the
beautiful girls." That included Diana and Eunice's sister, Eleanor Clark, who would soon marry a secretary
of Trotsky's to get him U.S. citizenship. It was said to
have been a "white" marriage, like Auden's with Erika
Mann. Pretentious, I thought. I didn't like Eleanor
Clark, and we barely acknowledged each other, though
we belonged politically to the same circle and had been
a class apart at Vassar. She was Lockwood, needless
to say. While I was married to John, she was with an
intelligent misanthrope named Herbert Solow. It
amused me to think that the self-absorbed Eleanor was
paired with a "Mr. Solo."

By the summer's end the "boys"—as the two *PR*
editors came to be called by their staff—were looking
for an office for the magazine, and I was looking for
an apartment for Philip and me. Thanks to a friend of
Lois Howland's, I found one on East End Avenue—
quite pretty and only moderately expensive. For Philip,
it was too far uptown; he clung to his Eighth Street
ways. And perhaps also too close to Yorkville, an
enclave of Germans, i.e., Nazis. But he bore it with
good grace. Nathalie Swan, still studying architecture,
helped us with furnishing advice—a room-divider to
make two rooms out of the long, narrow living-room,
and bookcases that would be built along one wall by
a carpenter and that I could stain myself. Philip and I
bought our furniture at Macy's. I remember a tall, very
"contemporary" steel lamp, and it must have been on

East End Avenue that I first owned the very square, bright red love seat that followed me for years to my various domiciles. There was an easy chair covered with gray tweed that went with Philip. When we split up—oh wellaway!—we divided the furniture. But that had not happened yet. No. After we moved to East End Avenue, into a ground-floor apartment across from Gracie Mansion, we had months still together, months in which I took the 86th Street crosstown bus and transferred to the Madison Avenue bus to get to work at Covici-Friede, on 32nd and Fourth, and came home by the same route at five, stopping in Yorkville to buy meat and groceries for the dinner I would cook that night.

It was a tight schedule: living on East End Avenue was highly impractical for me, while for Philip it was only a reason to grumble. Yet it was I who had chosen to do it, so I could not complain. We took walks in the park, and if we were approached by a beggar, Philip explained to me why charity was an error: the working-class needed to sharpen the contradictions of capitalism. At night or over the weekend I would write my theatre pieces, to come out monthly in the magazine—the boys had made me the theatre critic, not trusting my critical skills in other fields. They also gave me the job of translating Gide's *Retour de l'U.R.S.S.*, his second thoughts on the Soviet Union, which were going to come out in our second number. Sometimes Philip would pick me up at the Covici office, and we would go for drinks to the Vanderbilt Hotel, where they served you great trays of hot hors d'oeuvres free; you could eat enough over two cocktails to be able to skip supper. One day he brought along the young, high-cheekboned Delmore Schwartz, his latest find. On Saturday mornings, if I did not have to work, I could go down to the magazine for editorial meetings with the boys and Dwight and Fred and George Morris, our backer. Then we would all have lunch at Pete's Tavern on Irving Place or at a cheaper spot off Union Square. Now and then Philip and I would have people to dinner, and I cooked. I remember an evening with Bill Troy and his wife, Léonie Adams, and Troy's lecturing us over pre-dinner Tom Collinses on the difference between symbolism and allegory—symbolism, good; allegory, bad—a burning subject with him. Troy, who was about to begin teaching at Bennington, was an arrogant Irish puritan of the type I imagined Joyce to be; I could picture him leaning on an ashplant.

I was conscious of the discrepancy between Philip's working time and mine. Philip's day consisted of dropping in at the magazine, arguing with whoever was there, reading the mail, directing the composition of the "Editorial Statement" that would lay down the line of the new *PR*, and writing an occasional book review for *The Nation*. He had to check in every weekday at the Writers' Project, but that was a formality —necessary to draw the relief check. There he used to encounter types like Norbert Guterman, whom he had known in Party circles—*Luftmenschen*, he called them. My slight resentment of my heavier load was tempered by the sense of being noble and by pride in being able to do as much as I did. We quarreled but much less than we had. Now the bone of contention was our difference in religion—a curious thing to be angry about, since both of us were atheists. No doubt it was another disguise for the class war.

I discovered that Philip had never read the Gospels. Nor, for that matter, our Christian Old Testament. To me this came as a shock, all the more so as it made one wonder how he had managed to understand Eliot, one of his favorite modern masters. Even before Eliot's religious phase, there must have been problems. "Ash Wednesday"? *The Waste Land?* The grail? For once, Philip concurred. I was right, he agreed, and there was also Joyce, who, though not a believer, used the Christian myth. The last word made me bridle, despite his conciliatory intention. Did he think the Crucifixion was a *myth?* In any case, we came to an agreement. He promised that he would read the whole Bible if I would leave him in peace. I do not remember whether that included the Acts and the Epistles.

The amazing thing was that Philip did it. It took him a full week, but he enjoyed it. Naturally, while he was doing that, he could not be expected to do anything else. *My* Bible was his alibi for inactivity, and, recognizing it, we both laughed. As a penance, I may have taught him the Seven Deadly Sins, with emphasis on Sloth. One of Philip's great charms was that he truly loved to learn. Being impressionable, he could not fail to respond to the beauty of the King James version. All this was part of our love for each other; the shadows that fell across our relationship were still mainly an effect of social differences. For example, he did not like my insistence on our having a drink before dinner every single night—even in Reno, alone, I had had two Singapore Slings at the Riverside Inn before having dinner at my boarding-house. He analyzed my dependence on it as a class thing. Or our having to have a tablecloth and napkins and my mother's silver for just the two of us at supper. But he learned to help with the dishes, which he had never done before.

On my side, I loved hearing about his Russian childhood. His parents had been storekeepers in a village in the Ukraine; his grandmother lived with them. They were educated people—Zionists, as I said—and spoke Russian. He remembered one day when his grandmother came home with the terrible announcement, "The Tsar has fallen," and to him and his mother it was as if she had said "The sky has fallen." He hurried to hide behind the counter or under his grandmother's skirts. For several days they stayed in the house, fearfully, and this happened more than once during the civil war, as their village was taken and retaken by Reds and Whites and the people hid from both. Toward the end of the war, his family emigrated.

He remembered a time in Austria—his first acquaintance with German—and, after that, Palestine, and his father's furniture factory—in Joppa, I think it was—where the workers were Arabs. He felt a sympathy for them—the beginning of radicalization?—noting that they ate and slept and prayed lined up against the walls of the big room they worked in; if they had wives and family, they had left them behind. Out of his young boy's sense of an alien worker caste, separated from him by language and religion, a view of Israel was slowly worked out that was more complex than that of most New York Jews.

In Palestine, Philip had learned some Hebrew, and he liked to tell the story of the implantation of Hebrew in Palestine by a certain forceful rabbi who was an early settler. This rabbi decided one morning to compel his fellow settlers to forsake the corrupt high German (Yiddish) of the East European ghettoes that was the only common language they had. He began to speak Hebrew to anyone who addressed him and would hear only Hebrew when replied to by his co-religionists. If they answered him in Yiddish, the rabbi admonished them in Hebrew, "Jew, speak Jewish!" Since the rabbi was an important figure whom many people wanted to talk with, the whole Zionist settlement was forced to learn Hebrew from one day to the next. I suppose this was a fable based on a core of truth, but it pleased me to believe it literally since it gave Philip such deep delight.

Another of Philip's charms was the tenderness of his feeling for the Jewish state and its short history. Unlike most of the other Jewish intellectuals around *PR*, he was exempt from what is known as Jewish self-hatred. Philip loved being Jewish, so that if one cared for him one came to love that bit of him, too. This may have been related to his love for his mother, which had kept him sweet, at bottom, underneath his sourness. His given name was Ilya Greenberg; the authorities on New York intellectuals say "Ivan," which I feel sure is wrong. It is true that "Ilya" does not translate into "Philip," but neither does "Ivan," which would lead to "John" or "Hans." "Ilya," I guess, could be "Elijah" or "Elias," either one more appropriate. "Rahv," his pseudonym, chosen, of course, by him, means rabbi in Hebrew.

Though prone to shout when in polemical vein, he had a soft voice, rather breathy, with a touch of a whisper in it. In speaking English, he never lost his Russian accent and could never pronounce the letter "h"—there is no "h" in Russian. A nice story is told of him at a later period: a young writer had submitted a piece of fiction to the magazine based on the Gian-Carlo Menotti–Sam Barber household; Philip rejected it, instructing the young author categorically, "*Partisan Review* is an 'eterosexual magazine. It does not publish 'omosexual stories."

The magazine's initials were usually held to stand for "Philip Rahv." I am not sure whether Philip, at the beginning, was aware of this identity. I doubt it, because when we were trying to find a new name to go with the magazine's new politics, we spent many hours discussing it at Brookfield Center and nobody mentioned the coincidence of the original name with Philip's initials. In the end, we kept the name. The word "partisan," which we all liked, had surely been thought up by Philip. I can hear it now, pronounced in his caressing voice, as I can hear his highest term of praise, "modern." Another adjective, this one derogatory, comes back to me in William Phillips's nasal Brooklyn tones—"home-made." I do not know why this should be an injurious description of anything, but perhaps William, as a Marxist, felt that ideas and theories ought to be factory-produced. He would have been unaware of the usual application to cakes and candies.

Philip's eventual mother-in-law, a founder of the Junior League, liked to say of him to her friends: "Yes, isn't it remarkable, he got his education in our great public-library system!" That was true. He certainly read Marx and much else in U.S. public libraries. "Philip's alma mater," Fred Dupee is supposed to have quipped on passing the lions of the 42nd Street branch.

About his public-school experiences in Providence, Rhode Island, I am a bit hazy. I know he lived there with his older brother before and after his time in Palestine and was sent to grade school wearing long pants. As a little boy in those long pants, he must have started to speak English; he remembered trying to look up the teacher's skirts. After a period in high school, getting Americanized, somehow he got to Portland, Oregon, and found a job in advertising, coining catchy names for products. When the Depression struck, he drifted back east, where he became acquainted with breadlines and Central Park benches as well as the New York Public Library on 42nd Street. What he saw and read made a convinced Marxist of him. He joined the New York branch of the John Reed Clubs, where he met William Phillips (alias Wallace Phelps), a former student of Sidney Hook's at New York University, and the result was *Partisan Review*.

That story is told in a number of memoirs and intellectual histories of the time. John Strachey is said to have given a boost to the new magazine (conceived as an organ of the John Reed Clubs) by donating the take of a public lecture he undertook for the purpose. This must have been when I met him at the beer party in Eunice Rodman's backyard—during his triumphal visit to the U.S. Otherwise my recollections tend to differ from the now canonical versions. For example, as I remember it, Philip said that William had been in the Party (hence "Wallace Phelps," his Party name) and he himself had not—a strange fluke of chance, he thought, as he was as much of a Party-liner as William, probably more. In the memoir William has written, it is the other way around. Perhaps my memory of what Philip said is wrong. But then, how does William explain "Wallace Phelps"?

None of the histories I've looked at tells how I happened to be on the magazine. I am not sure myself, but I suspect that Philip imposed me on the others. And they were not altogether pleased. It was not that they thought poorly of me. At least Fred and Dwight didn't, as far as I know. But they resented the blunt exercise of Philip's will. Yet possibly poor Philip was only responding to pressure applied by me. Until the archives are opened (as we said then), we shall never find out. Dwight, it occurs to me, was in no position to cast the first stone, having himself imposed Nancy as business manager. But on that score, I recall no grumbling, not until Dwight moved the magazine to his apartment, where he could have everything under his and Nancy's control. But that was later.

Yet before we get to that later, which is coming ineluctably anyway, let me pause and go back to that summer, before we moved uptown to the Bregmans' apartment, before East End Avenue. What do I remember, besides what I have just been telling? Well, I suddenly hear my voice speaking in a rather affected tone, as though I thought I was Hope Williams in an Arthur Hopkins comedy. "My dear, I've got the most *Lev*antine lover." I am in Nathalie Swan's apartment —she had moved out of her family's house—and I am telling her about Philip, with whom I have fallen in love. That is what, in a mode of extreme sophistication, that sentence is trying to say. Perhaps I am only telling it to her in her own patois. It was around that time that her wearied New York "social" voice remarked to me, "Oh, dear, Father's getting rich again."

Next, Philip and I are on the terrace of the Brevoort Hotel. It is after dinner, and we have ordered a pitcher of beer—an inexpensive way of spending an evening on lower Fifth Avenue watching the people go by. Someone has joined us, drawing a chair up to our table. It is Herbert Solow (the "Mr. Solo" I spoke of), and we are discussing Roosevelt's appointment of Justice Hugo Black to the Supreme Court. Philip and I are taking this calmly, but Solow is excited. "But the fellow is a *Klans*man!" We are impressed by the seriousness of this worldly, saturnine man. He has been in Coyoacán with Trotsky and has had an affair with Adelaide Walker, well qualified by her beauty to be a Trotskyite. Before the summer is over, he will have the nerve to ask me to go riding with him in his two-seater, without reference to Philip, with whom I am living and who has answered the phone. I told him I couldn't.

Then an evening at the Jumble Shop, on 8th Street, with Filipino waiters. Philip is haranguing me about formalism and Paul Valéry, and I do not understand very well. He talks about *Le Cimetière Marin*. Some of his friends join us—Lionel Abel and William? Perhaps Harold Rosenberg. I cannot make out whether they are for formalism or against it, or whether they disagree among themselves. It would seem to me that if Philip is so violently opposed to socialist realism, he ought to be in favor of what sounds like its opposite. Yet the word "formalism" as they pronounce it sounds condemnatory. In fact what was happening was a slow change of mind. Denunciation of formalism went back to the Bolshevik doctrinal creed, and, once the "boys" had broken with Stalinism in politics, should no longer have incurred their ire; for Americans, the concept had been a Procrustean bed all along. The discussion in the Jumble Shop was almost a valedictory.

Meanwhile, the Moscow trials continued; the Spanish Republic was tottering, thanks to non-intervention, though we could still claim some victories. The second Moscow trial—Radek and Pyatakov—had taken place in January; again confessions were followed by executions as the revolution devoured its own children. In June, the great civil war hero Marshal Tukhachevsky and several lesser Red Army generals were secretly tried and executed as Hitler agents; this coincided with the second meeting of the Writers' Congress—"pimples on the smiling face of the Soviet Union." But a real and terrible coincidence, which, as they say, was "no coincidence," was with the disappearance and probable execution of Andrés Nin in Spain; as is now recognized, the two occurrences were related.

A thrill of horror had shot through our group when we heard what had happened, *unbelievably*, to Tukhachevsky. Emotionally, we did not mind so much the fates of Zinoviev and Kamenev, Radek and Pyatakov, and (soon to come) Bukharin—Old Bolsheviks, all of them, *civilians*, brain workers like ourselves, not heroes many times decorated, of the Red Army. Our feelings on this subject were strangely mixed, I think; at any rate, mine were. On the one hand, grief and horror; on the other, exultation. The liquidation of Tukhachevsky, we saw, would be fatal for Stalinism, as indeed it nearly proved to have been, in a military sense, when Hitler in 1941 broke the non-aggression pact and invaded: the Red Army, after the bloody destitution of its leaders in 1937, let itself be overrun. Of course we could not see that far ahead, but we sensed that Stalin had overreached himself when he moved against the Red Army. Thus we jubilated in being shown to be right; still, Tukhachevsky's murder could not make us happy—on the contrary. Much more than I, Philip grieved, I suspect; a boyish part of him was proudly invested in the Red Army. The Nazi-Soviet Pact, when it came, must have had a similar effect on him, validating his arguments and paining his soul. During those years he told Fred Dupee that he sometimes woke up in the night, sweating; the question that jerked him awake was "And what if Stalin is right?"

Now I come to a moment that can still make *me* flinch more than fifty years later. A premonition of worse to come might have been registered by both of us on the night we went to a big party in a strange apartment somewhere uptown. We are living on East End Avenue. Philip is wearing a new suit, very becoming in purplish browns, which we bought him at Altman's. Many prominent Trotskyists are present at the party, known to me mostly by name. Among them, lounging on a sofa, is Max Eastman, the editor of *The Masses* and the old *Liberator*, who had nearly been lynched for his principles during the First World War—we had had his *Enjoyment of Poetry* with Miss Kitchel in freshman English. This white-haired spell-binder, the son of preachers from Canandaigua, New York, was handsome, tall, all his life a fascinator of women. His film on the Russian Revolution, *From the Tsar to Lenin*, was just being shown. In sum, all I remember is what I would like to forget: having had a lot of drinks, sitting on Max Eastman's lap; out of a corner of memory's eye, I see Philip's face. The next morning he was still very angry with me. I had an awful hangover and had to stay home from work for two whole days. That was all. Eventually Philip forgave. I did not see Eastman again for many years. Once was at his house at Croton with Charlie Chaplin, and the second time was at a conference at the Waldorf on cultural freedom—he had become a right-winger and upheld Joe McCarthy.

Nonetheless, the stage was set, all right. On the wall of our life together hung a gun waiting to be fired in the final act. In Seattle, my grandfather would soon die (December 30), aged seventy-nine, which, according to a series of psychoanalysts, deprived me of a "father figure." But Grandpa was still alive, going to his office and playing his daily golf game, when I first met my fate, in the *PR* office late on a Saturday morning (I must have worked that Saturday at Covici). I appeared in my best clothes—a black silk dress with tiers of fagoting and, hung from my neck, a long, large silver fox fur—having been told by Philip that Edmund Wilson would be dropping in at the magazine and we would all take him to lunch. My partly bare arms tell me that it would have been a fall day. We were all on hand for the big occasion; we were hoping for a contribution from him for our first or second number and we wanted to make a good impression, although my costume, as I look back on it and as I sensed even at the time, was more suited to a wedding reception than to a business meeting in the offices of a radical magazine.

THREE

He bustled into our office, short, stout, middle-aged, breathy—born May 8, 1895; we others were in our twenties—with popping reddish-brown eyes and fresh pink skin, which looked as though he had just bathed. Perhaps it was this suggestion of baths—the tepidarium—and his fine straight nose that gave him a Roman air. I think he was wearing a gray two-piece suit and a white shirt.

We walked to the Union Square restaurant and took a table on the second floor, above the cafeteria. I was the only woman, but Wilson did not seem to notice me specially. He talked mainly to Dwight and Fred. Somebody asked for our drink order. We were all, except for Dwight perhaps, nervous and tongue-tied, and a drink would have helped. But Wilson shook his head irritably, as though annoyed by the proposal, and we all meekly followed suit. Probably he didn't drink and disapproved of the habit. Maybe one of the boys had the courage to order a beer.

That is all I recall of this first meeting. Of course I remembered him from Vassar in my junior year—the year after *Axel's Castle*—when he had read a paper on Flaubert with such alarming pauses that Miss Sandison, who had introduced him, had run down to the basement in Avery to find him a glass of water: *"Vox exhaurit in faucibus,"* she said later. Now he showed more aplomb as we talked about the new, anti-Stalinist *PR* and what we were going to have in our first issues. He agreed that we ought to have something by Trotsky, if we could get it. He may have tried to interest us in his friend Paul Rosenfeld, to be our music critic. We spoke of André Gide and his revised view of the USSR, exemplified in the piece I was translating for our second number. Wilson had read it in French, he said, cutting the subject off. As I later learned, he did not think much of Gide. The conversation turned to *Travels in Two Democracies*, which had described his own trip to Russia, contemporaneous with Gide's. The title showed how far he had come politically in a little more than a year; that book had been published in 1936. He could no longer call Russia a democracy unless ironically—the trials had happened in between. Essentially his book belonged to the epoch of the Kirov assassination, and perhaps he was slightly embarrassed by his failure to see ahead.

Over lunch, his voice was light and pleasant; this was not one of his booming days. He was always at his best when he was bookish. By the time we separated, he had promised us a piece for our first number. The following week Margaret Marshall called me at Covici. She had heard from Wilson, who wanted to take us out to dinner, the two of us. She supposed it was because of *The Nation* series, in which he had been singled out for praise. If so, it seemed odd that he had waited two years, I thought. Peggy, who had met him, was being coy about why he was asking us both, when he "kind of" liked her, she was sure. Perhaps he wanted chaperonage, I suggested lightly. For my part, I could not guess what was in his mind. The whole thing seemed very strange. But if Wilson was "after" one of us, it must be me, I reasoned, since he had just met me in the *PR* office. Fred and the boys puzzled over the invitation, too, when they learned of it. I wondered—maybe we all wondered—whether Wilson knew that I was Philip's girl.

As the date for the dinner approached, my co-editors did quite a bit of worrying and wondering. Yet nobody, including Philip, thought I should decline. With our high ambitions for the magazine, we could not consider that. Instead, we worried about me. The boys did not hide their fear that my political inexperience could make the magazine look foolish to that experienced older critic who knew such a great deal about Marxism and the U.S. social scene. And I was literary in the wrong way, not really *modern*, still interested in graduate-student stuff like Shakespeare and the Elizabethans. I was not as big a liability as George Morris; he had gone into the Workers Bookstore and asked for a copy of Trotsky's *The Revolution Betrayed,* wearing spats and carrying a cane! He had been curious to read it, he said, having heard so much talk about it in the office, and had thought that a neighborhood bookstore with "Workers" in the name would be a good place to find it, never dreaming that it was the official Party place. Even after hearing this explanation, the boys were aghast. I knew better than that, of course, but I was politically undeveloped, prone to wonder whether the Tsar and his family *needed* to be killed. Clearly it nettled my fellow editors that I had been singled out to represent the magazine—why not one of *them?* With their excitable apprehensions, most evident in Philip and William, they were making me fearful myself of what I might say or do. There could be no reprieve: Wilson had called Margaret Marshall again to confirm the date and tell us to meet him at Mary's—an Italian restaurant deep in the Village known to his generation.

At this point Fred Dupee came to my rescue. Since it looked as if the great critic did not drink, I would need some bucking up for the ordeal ahead, he decided, seeing me white and strained in my "dinner dress," when I stopped by the office for a last-minute briefing. So he took me to the Hotel Albert bar, on University Place, and ordered Daiquiris, my favorite cocktail at the time. I must have had three.

Wilson and Peggy were already at Mary's, in an upstairs private dining-room. Far from not drinking, he was ordering a second round of double Manhattans when I arrived. Naturally I took one, then a second, without saying that I had already had drinks with Fred. But if I had, it would have made no difference. Wilson was in a bibulous mood. And I learned why he had said no to drinks before lunch that day in the Union Square restaurant: he had had a colossal hangover, and the hair of the dog was not one of his weaknesses.

His habit, as I came to know, was to get thoroughly soused (which we were on our way to doing at Mary's), then sleep it off and turn over a new leaf the next day on arising. Bathed and shaved, clad in snowy linen—he wore B.V.D.s—he emerged from his toilet reborn, or like a risen god. That he did not smoke probably helped. The glowing pink man we had taken to lunch was a resurrected Wilson, who had harried hell the night before. The boys, who had read *I Thought of Daisy* (I had not), might have guessed that the respected critic was no teetotaler.

After the double Manhattans, we drank dago red and finally B. & B. This was a favorite potion with Wilson, which I never came to like; for me, the sweetness of the Benedictine spoiled the taste of the brandy. All that liquor loosened my tongue, and I had what was called a talking jag. Since Wilson seemed interested, I told them the story of my life: Seattle, the flu, the death of my parents, Minneapolis, and certainly quite a bit about Uncle Myers, not omitting, I fear, the razor strop. . . . Then, somehow, we were at the Chelsea Hotel, on West 23rd Street. Possibly we had dropped in on Ben Stolberg, who was living there at the time. I was no longer very conscious of Margaret Marshall, but she was still one of the party. Fairly soon, I hope, I "passed out."

As I learned the next day, my inert form put them in a quandary. Neither Peggy nor Wilson knew where I lived. Ben Stolberg would not have known either. If they had tried looking in the phone book, they would not have found me—Philip and I had only recently moved in. Wilson, though no doubt very drunk, rose to the occasion. He took a room for himself—he was living in the country, near Stamford—and another for Margaret and me.

Opening an eye the morning after, I looked cautiously across to the next bed, having assessed that I was in a twin-bedded room. With an episode like the one with the man in the Brooks Brothers shirt behind me, I had reason to fear the worst. In the other bed, a yawning Margaret Marshall opened her eyes. There was no one else in the room, so far as I could see, and I guessed that we were in a hotel. I let a cry escape me, a loud groan or moan. It was the same awful certainty speaking that had just awakened me, like a voice in my ear: "Oh, God, oh, God, I've disgraced *Partisan Review*." In my slip, I cried hopelessly while she looked on. Wilson must have gone back to Stamford. At any rate, we did not see him that morning. Doubtless he had paid our bill.

My first action, of course, was mandatory: call Philip. Maybe Peggy was kind enough to get the number for me when she saw how scared I was. They knew each other because he wrote reviews for her, for *The Nation*, but this was the first she knew of our living together. Anyway, while we were still in that hotel room, she talked to him. She told him that I had passed out and that Wilson, not knowing what to do with me, had persuaded her to stay with me in the Chelsea in the next bed. Philip believed her. Angry as he was, he felt pity for me. Either he came down in a taxi to get me or I took a taxi home by myself. I was still wearing my "dinner dress." Either way, he forgave me. It was the second time, counting the Eastman's-lap folly. I was horrified to think of the night he must have spent, not knowing what had happened to me. Probably he blamed Fred when he heard about the Daiquiris. But as the helmsman of a young, endangered periodical, he would not have allowed himself to be angry with Wilson.

Philip's capacity for forgiveness will surprise people who thought of him (and wrote of him) as a gruff, rancorous man. But it is a fact and not to be fully explained by the strong attraction between us. In another man, this could have led to a fierce, jealous resentment. But Philip had an open heart and a childish, somewhat docile nature with those he had opened it to, few as they were. That he could accept my penitence—and not from any weakness—must have meant that he understood that I loved him. I did, and still do, vividly, as I write these words. Real love, said Hannah Arendt, is mutual. It is something that happens between two people. After much reflection, I agree with that. The other thing, the thing you read about in Proust, is *infatuation* (from *fatuus*, "foolish"); it is much commoner than love, and you can get over it. Years later, when Philip died and I wrote a little obituary on him, Hannah, on reading it, was astonished. "So, my dear, you loved him. I never knew." Maybe, till she said it, I had not known it myself.

Another way of reconciling the common view of Philip held by his enemies—i.e., by most of the males of the *PR* circle—with my own experience of him is that he *became* unforgiving after what I did to his childlike heart. I *hope* it is not that.

What I have to relate now is painful to tell. To put it "as in a nutshell" (as Hannah, now dead, too, used to say), Philip still had a lot of forgiving to do. I mean forgiving of me. The next occasion was another dinner with Wilson. Again he asked the two of us, Peggy and me, as though we were wedded by our collaboration in his not very flexible mind, and again we accepted and again the scene was Mary's. Again Philip did not interpose a veto. This time I did not have Daiquiris to prepare me and this time I did not pass out. Alas, no. Instead, after the B. & B.s, the three of us rode in a taxi all the way out to Stamford, where Wilson lived in a house he rented from Margaret De Silver (Baldwin Locomotive, the American Civil

Liberties Union, Carlo Tresca) on the Mianus River. Fittingly, the house was named Trees. Again we did not call Philip, not, at any rate, till the next morning, when I conveyed an invitation from Wilson to take a train at Grand Central and join us. *And Philip did.*

At Trees, at one end of the colorless living-room, we had a lunch cooked by an old black maid named Hattie, who occupied a wing of the house with her grandchildren. Wilson was affable; probably he served Liebfraumilch, his preferred table wine after Château d'Yquem, and we talked about books and writers. Then Philip took me home on the train. I cannot remember what happened to Margaret Marshall. Perhaps she took an earlier train back, for I do not see her sharp little face or hear her thin voice at the lunch table. Could she have gone to see her friend and contributor Franz Hollering, who lived with his Czech movie-actress wife in a house on the Eitingon property? Yes, the same name the reader has heard about in the first chapter, in connection with Clifford Odets, Johnsrud, and Frank Merlin; Motty Eitingon, a fur importer, had ties with the Soviet Union. In any event, while Miss Marshall slept in a little guest room just down the hall, I had gone to bed with Wilson.

Yes. That had not been my intention when I followed him into his study (book-lined, of course) to continue, as I drunkenly thought, a conversation we were having. I greatly liked talking to him but was not attracted to him sexually. He was too old and too fat. Nevertheless, when he firmly took me into his arms, misunderstanding my intention, I gave up the battle. On the couch in the study, we drunkenly made love.

Some time before daylight, I left him and returned to the room that was supposed to be mine. I don't think I saw him alone till many days later. At breakfast, produced by Hattie, we made no reference to what had happened. I called Philip, and we waited for him to come. It was only then, I believe, that Wilson understood that I lived with Philip. When he started to write to me, it was always to my office.

One day, a bit afterward, when we were finally able to talk—I had come out to Trees on the train, and we did not drink—I tried to explain to him my motives in returning to his study that night. But he would not listen to what I felt sure was the truth; only facts spoke to him, and the fact was that I had let him make love to me. Again, I gave up. You cannot argue against facts. And yet to this very day I am convinced that he had me wrong: I only wanted to talk to him. The reader will find an echo of this in Chapter Five of *A Charmed Life*, where Martha Sinnott, happily remarried, looks back on her first husband, the awful Miles Murphy: "She did not understand what had happened. She had only, she bemoaned, wanted to talk to him—a well-known playwright and editor, successful, positive, interested in her ideas and life-history." (Let the reader be warned: *A Charmed Life*, though derived, like all books, from experience, is not an autobiographical novel, and Miles Murphy must not be taken for a disguised portrait of Wilson. Martha, I admit, is a bit like me—I tried to change her and failed, as I failed later with Domna Rejnev in *The Groves of Academe*.) Maybe, when I wrote *A Charmed Life*, I was fooling myself about Martha's motives and am still fooling myself today, when I should be old enough to know better, about what drove me into Wilson's study on that long-ago night. At present, my guess is that it was the unwillingness to end an evening that gets hold of people who have been drinking—*anything*, sex included, to avoid retiring. But that is a far cry from Wilson's fond persuasion.

Whatever the truth was, that I did not confess to Philip what had happened during that night at Trees indicated that a relationship with Wilson was beginning. The two of us had a secret between us, and Philip became the outsider. In my office at Covici, sitting opposite the ever-disapproving Miss Broene, I embarked on a correspondence with Wilson. He wrote, and I answered. His letters to me are at Vassar; mine to him are at Yale. Reading mine over, I am surprised by the intimacy and friendliness of my tone. There is a note of tenderness and teasing. Apparently I liked him much more than I remember, more than I ever would again. What I hear in the letters is not love, though—I never loved Wilson—but sympathy, affection, friendship. Later, I grew to think of him as a monster; the minotaur, we called him in the family, Bowden [Broadwater] and I. The comparison is exact (he was even related to the Bull family on his mother's side), and I may have felt a kind of friendship for the poor minotaur in his maze, so sadly dependent on the yearly sacrifice of maidens. But if, sensing that need, I warmed to Wilson, solitary among his trees, I did not guess that I would be one of the Athenian maidens with never a Theseus to rescue me.

If I had no premonition of what was in store, he, on his side, was hell-bent on my marrying him. He needed a wife "the worst way," to use one of his expressions, having lost his second, Margaret Canby, in a fall down some steep stairs five years before. The women he had been having affairs with were either unwilling to marry him or unsuited to the job or both. When I met him, he must have been desperate. He could not take care of himself; the old black woman, Hattie, was a kind of nurse to him. Herbert Solow used to tell a story of arriving at Trees for a call during this time and hearing Wilson's voice boom: "Hattie, Hattie! Where are my drawers?" He meant his underwear—those light lawn one-piece B.V.D.s he wore. He was comically dependent on old-fashioned terms. His bicycle was always "my wheel." Had he owned or driven a car, it would have been "the machine." His sexual organ, as readers of *Hecate County* discovered, was "my club": "My club was pressing through the tight confines of my evening dress."

No, I did not want to marry him. As a radical, I was against marriage. What happened is explained in *A Charmed Life*, in an analysis of the motive behind Martha's first marriage. "The fatalistic side of her character accepted Miles as a punishment for the sin of having slept with him when she did not love him, when she loved, she still felt, someone else. Nevertheless, she had naively sought a compromise. She had begged Miles merely to live with him, as his mistress." That was what I tried to sell Wilson on, quite nobly, I thought. But he was not interested. "I've had that," he replied, without elaboration. So finally I agreed to marry him as my punishment for having gone to bed with him—this was certainly part of the truth. As a modern girl, I might not have called that a "sin"; I thought in logical rather than in religious terms. The logic of having slept with Wilson compelled the sequence of marriage if that was what he wanted. Otherwise my action would have no consistency; in other words, no meaning. I could not accept the fact that I had slept with this fat, puffing man for no reason, simply because I was drunk. No. It had to make sense. Marrying him, though against my inclinations, *made* it make sense. There is something faintly Kantian here. But I did not know Kant then. Maybe I was a natural Kantian.

Of course, other reasons contributed. The death of my grandfather (as I have mentioned) may have been one. It was not that Wilson stood in as a father figure for me exactly, but he was an older man (there were seventeen years between us) and came from the same stock, Anglo-Saxon, Presbyterian. His father, like Grandpa, had been a distinguished lawyer—Attorney General of New Jersey under Governor Woodrow Wilson. There was a certain feeling of coming home, to my own people.

Then there were the intellectual attractions he offered, all of which were beyond Philip: we were going to read Juvenal together, for example. Also, there was the whole world of Nature and the outdoors, so closed to Philip. We were going to ride horses along the trails above the river; we were going to fish for trout. We would look for wild flowers in the woods: spring beauty, bloodroot, hepatica, trillium. Some of this we actually did. After we were married, we rode a few times, uninspiring horses; we caught perch and sunfish, if not trout, in the Mianus, and Edmund knew the wild flowers quite well. He taught me their names, for which I am still grateful. But we never read Juvenal.

It was an idyl he was offering me, and not wholly false. He, too, must have hoped that it would be like that. Probably I was stirred by memories of Lake Crescent and the morning walk to Marymere Falls, of Major Mathews and the spring woods near Tacoma. Those had been the happiest moments of my life. Though Wilson could furnish me no waterfalls, no carpets of violets, he had a wonderful gorge, I found, just up the river, with an icy green transparent pool at the bottom.

I loved that. His own anticipation must have centered on having an intellectual girl for a wife—the first one. After a protracted siege to Edna Millay, he had been "stuck on" the poet Léonie Adams. But Léonie had cared about women (Margaret Mead had been his principal rival), and now she was married to Bill Troy.

Besides the inducements of a shared classical education and the outdoors, he offered me the promise that marrying him would "do something" for me, that is, for my literary gift. "Rahv doesn't *do* anything for you," he argued, meaning that Rahv was slothfully content to have me do those theatre columns, which, according to Wilson, were not up to my real measure. "You draw a crushing brief against a play," he said. I did not exactly see what was wrong with that, but in fact he had put his finger on a limitation. I was not as narrow as Sidney Hook but I did treat most of the authors I wrote about as though they were under indictment. The tendency, evidently, was aggravated by Trotskyism. It was Wilson's belief that I ought not to be writing criticism—I had a talent, he thought, for imaginative writing. This was the opposite of what dear Miss Kitchel had decided for me at Vassar.

Looking back, I can see that he was right where Philip was concerned. If it had been left to Rahv, I never would have written a single "creative" word. And I do not hold it against him; on the contrary. His love, unlike Wilson's, was from the heart. He cared for what I was, not for what I might evolve into.

Whatever I might be *made* to be, with skillful encouragement, did not interest him. To say this today may seem hard on Wilson, as well as ungrateful on my part for what he did, in the first months of our marriage, to push me into "creativity." If he had not shut the door firmly on the little room he had shepherded me into (the same room Margaret Marshall had slept in), I would not be the "Mary McCarthy" you are now reading. Yet, awful to say, I am not particularly grateful.

At the time, I was not swayed by the argument of what he, compared with Philip, could do for me. It seemed mercenary. The picture of a powerful man trying with various baits and lures to rob a weaker man of his chief treasure was not very appealing. But Wilson never saw that angle. He saw what he perceived as my self-interest, to be furthered by my marriage to him. From the outside, however, things looked different. I remember that somebody of the *PR* circle —Delmore or Harold Rosenberg—was widely quoted as saying that Mary left Philip for Wilson because Wilson had a better prose style. I am not sure that Wilson did, or not always, and it would have been a bad reason, had it been operative, which of course it was not. My own explanation (if I must give but a single one) for my yielding to Wilson is the Marxist explanation. It was the same old class struggle that Philip and I had been waging from the moment we fell in love.

Wilson, relatively speaking, was upper class. That was all there was to it. Though he commanded a higher word rate, he was scarcely better heeled than Philip on the WPA. Wilson made more money, which he spent on taxis, liquor, long-distance phone calls. There was nothing left for clothes or furniture or jewelry, all of which I cared about. He could not do without taxis, booze, the long-distance telephone, and hence regarded them in the light of necessities. Another addiction (I almost forgot) was book-binding, which was just then beginning to take hold of him. In terms of wealth, he was hard to situate. Though he could seldom pay the phone bill without hasty recourse to his mother, you could not call him poor, since he always had enough to eat. Neither could you say he was rich.

One material inducement that counted in the decision I was being pressed to make was his promise that we would have children. Philip was in no position to offer that; he was still not free to marry, lacking the price of a divorce, and he was not keen on the idea of progeny even in later life, when he was free and could afford it—he never had any children. But Wilson made good on that. He took me to New York in a taxi for my lying-in, though we had no clothes of our own for the newborn Reuel. My friend Florine Katz gave me her baby clothes, rubber pants, and diapers; her baby scales, I think, too. Wilson's mother had to be appealed to for the baby carriage when we were leaving the hospital. Once we were back home, the

Bathinette gave rise to a crisis (he thought we didn't need one), and I forget how we managed for a playpen. No doubt it was old Mrs. Wilson once again to the rescue.

But I am going too fast. There was a time when I had not yet agreed to marry him but was taking the train out to Stamford and the milk train back while Philip, somehow, remained in ignorance. I also met Wilson at least once for dinner in New York, and there was some question of a showing of *Snow White and the Seven Dwarfs* (his choice). As he continued to "press his suit," each time I managed a stolen meeting—once I pretended to have gone to a prize fight (with Mannie, I suppose)—I was risking the unthinkable: Philip's discovery. Possibly I hoped that the affair with Wilson would come to an end all by itself somehow, thus relieving me of having to tell Philip.

Well, finally I told him. Wilson was "at" me to do it, till one night I did. But before I go ahead with that melancholy story, I must make a confession. Since starting this chapter I have been rereading the letters I wrote on Covici-Friede Inc. stationery to "Mr. Edmund Wilson, Westover Road, Stamford, Connecticut." And they tell me, among other things, that Peggy Marshall was very much present at lunch with Wilson on that morning after at Trees. Listen to this, from my second letter, written on a "Tuesday afternoon" in reply to one from him; the postmark is November 30, 1937:

"Sunday was a bad day for me. . . . When you took Peggy on your lap, something happened to my face that I couldn't stop. Philip leaned over to me and said, 'I know something about you,' and I said, 'I know you do,' and he said, 'You're jealous,' and I said, 'Yes.' He attributed it, however, to an extreme coquettishness, and didn't look further for explanations."

When he took Peggy on his lap, was he sitting at the table or was it on the sofa? Grotesque! Did he do it to throw Philip off the scent? If so, it was a good move. Incredibly, though the letters were going back and forth for more than a month and a half, right through Christmas, and I was meeting Wilson about once a week, Philip seems to have had no suspicion. How shameful a successful deception is! But maybe he was so secure in his own manhood that he was unable to think of Wilson as any kind of rival.

When at last I told him, after the first starts of surprise, he took the news very soberly. He was struck by the marriage proposal into a kind of thoughtfulness. It was as though the situation was too grave for anger. His big dark eyes with their prominent whites grew still, as if wounded. "What do you want to do, Mary?" he said gently. Probably I cried and told him that I didn't know: Wilson was in such a hurry; he was rushing me.

Obviously I don't remember the details of the conversation; probably there was more than one. Maybe I cooked our dinner in the middle of it. Or we went to bed and got up. The gist was that Philip begged me, for both our sakes, to take my time. He appeared to consider *for* me, like a more experienced brother. With Wilson, there was the age difference, he pointed out. And I was young enough to wait a while to have children. Before deciding anything I ought to talk it over with an older person, not my grandmother (she was too old) but someone who could be told that he and I were living together. Why not Nathalie Swan's mother, a society woman but rather intellectual?

Reluctantly, Wilson agreed that I could think about it. Late in January, I telephoned Mrs. Swan and went up to stay with her at the Swans' country house near Salisbury, Connecticut. Nathalie came along or followed in a day or two. Being the person I was, in the midst of my grief for Philip, I was excited by the momentousness of it all. Having such a big decision to mull over made me feel important. Mrs. Swan, no doubt, was flattered to be consulted; she was aware of Wilson as a literary figure. It did not subtract from the solemnity of the occasion to be waited on by a butler and maids, to drink Mrs. Swan's society Martini (gin and two vermouths) before lunch and Joe Swan's vintage wine with meals, and to have coffee with hot milk on my breakfast tray. In other words, I enjoyed myself. It was a long time since I had stayed in the Swan country house, where everything was perfect. Meanwhile, Philip waited for the result in our apartment. I don't recall where Wilson was. Probably he was besieging me with impatient telephone calls.

Mrs. Swan had the good sense to listen while remaining neutral. If she gave me any advice, it was "Wait a little longer." Yes! Precisely! But that was wise counsel I did not want to hear. To resist that advice was to precipitate myself into Wilson's arms. He understood that very well, though I did not. To this day, I can't make out whether I "really" wanted to marry Wilson or prayed to be spared it.

I took the train back from Salisbury. After that, I remember nothing till days later, when I was on the train with Edmund, going down to his mother's place in Red Bank, New Jersey. I had told Philip my decision, spent a few nights at Trees, had a Wassermann (or didn't you need a Wassermann in New Jersey?), quit my job, and was feeling miserable. I looked at the tall grasses outside the train window and looked the other way, into Wilson's closed face, the narrow lips set in a tight line. I do not know whether Philip and I had made love in our bed when I came back from staying at Salisbury. I hope so. Then had come the chilly day when we divided our possessions. I remember the result but not the painful event: Philip took the tall steel lamp and the tweed-covered armchair, as I've said; I took some boldly designed Italian plates, my mother's silver, and the red love seat, which stayed with me through two more marriages. Each took his own books. Did we have the 1911 *Britannica* or had that gone to Johnsrud?

Needless to say, Wilson and I were being married in a civil ceremony, at the Red Bank city hall. Our witnesses were two town employees. Afterward we went back to Edmund's mother's house. She was a stumpy downright old lady with an ear trumpet and a loud, deaf voice. She looked like a warthog, Bowden eventually decided, basing himself on my description and an illustration in *Webster's Collegiate*—he had never seen Mrs. Wilson nor an actual warthog in the flesh. But that was pretty much how she looked. Wilson inherited his body structure from her family, the Kimballs. His nose and forehead came from his father. At lunch—a pretty fruit jelly for dessert—I was introduced to Jenny, her companion, rather elderly herself, and to a cook and a driver. Mrs. Wilson was in the habit of sitting all day long at a living-room window of her sizable house on Vista Place, ticking off the people that had died in the houses across the street. This was *her* house. According to Edmund, her first words on watching her husband die in the house they had always lived in were "Now I can have my new house." She was a gruff personality who did not much approve of Edmund; he believed that she held it against him that his large head had torn her vaginal tissues as he was being born. There was not much love lost between them. Yet there was a kind of grumbly, unwilling attachment. They were more alike than they knew. When Dos Passos' beautiful wife, Katy, was decapitated in an automobile accident, Edmund's first remark, made after visiting Dos in the Boston hospital, was "Now he can get married and have some children."

He was dependent on his mother for money, because his father's estate (not large) had been left entirely to her. What Edmund saw as his rightful share she doled out to him as though it were bounty. Yet the fact was that the bulk of her capital was hers by family inheritance, wisely invested for her by a stockbroker brother, Edmund's uncle Win. She had a good head for money and rated her brothers higher than her husband.

One of her complaints about Edmund was his proneness to marry unsuitable women. She had already brought up a child of his first marriage, to the actress Mary Blair. When the little girl (according to Edmund) had been left by her mother in front of an open window while sick with the flu, he had removed her bodily to Red Bank and deposited her with his mother, where she remained till now. I did not meet Rosalind on the day of our wedding because she was fifteen and away at boarding-school. But her home was still Red Bank. His second wife, Margaret, was a drinker, his mother thought. And now he had married me.

After lunch, he left me to sit opposite the old lady and shout into her ear trumpet, while he himself climbed upstairs to "his" room to read or sleep. I was surprised when he did this on our first, newlywed visit, but I soon understood that it must have been his habit with all his wives: part of a wife's function was to address his mother's defective hearing. She appeared to like me well enough; the complaints she voiced to me about Edmund could be taken as a sign of friendship. I imagine that she handed him a nice check for a wedding present as we were leaving for New York. She gave me her cheek to kiss.

It had been arranged that in the evening he would meet two of my brothers in the bar of the New Weston Hotel, where we were spending our wedding night. Since neither of my brothers remembers anything of this except the fact that it happened, it looks as if it had gone all right. Kevin and Preston had come to New York from Minneapolis this January with a friend to try their luck, Kevin and the friend as actors, Preston as a photographer. They were living in a room on West 23rd Street and had very little money. It was Preston who got discouraged first and went home, where he got a little help from our uncle Lou in Minneapolis. Kevin hung on. On the day of the meeting with Wilson, all three still had hopes.

My brothers were both good-looking boys in the McCarthy way—dark hair, light eyes, long dark eyelashes. And of course they were shy as they talked of their plans. Wilson took no exception to them that I noticed while we were sitting with drinks—no more than two or three. But upstairs in the bedroom (this was our honeymoon), he suddenly burst out and told me my brothers were agents of the GPU. He was very drunk, more drunk than I had seen him before, and at first he did not make himself clear. He had started with innuendo, lurching on to accusation. I could not believe I was hearing right; it was some sort of joke, I guessed. When I finally knew he was serious, I was at a loss as to how to refute the charge, since I could not see what had led up to it. Even now, I still have no notion. I may guess that in the bar he had sensed a plot thickening against him: I had tricked him into marriage so as to deliver him to the GPU through these brothers of mine who were agents. He grunted some threats, but he did not hit me. Abruptly he fell asleep. I lay awake, silently weeping. The marriage was over, I had to assume.

In a sense that was true. It was the end of my high hopes for a "classical" life. No more idyl. The next morning is a blank for me. If I confronted him with "Why did you call my brothers GPU agents?" he evaded an answer with "Come along now; we have a train to catch," or something of the sort. If I said nothing, *he* said nothing. And he never reverted to the subject. When Kevin came out to Trees that spring to ask for help, he gave him a five-dollar bill. No mention to me of "Your brother, the agent." I suppose that the wedding night had brought on an access of paranoia —dread of being "tied down"? The political area at that time was highly sensitized. We both thought in those terms. Probably he saw me as a Trotskyite girl, the reverse, of course, of a Stalinist agent, but in hallucination extremes meet. Had he faced up the next day to what he had done, we might have been friends again, and the charge would have been reason for laughter: "I thought Mary's brothers were GPU agents." But perhaps he did not know me well enough to expose himself by an admission of error. In later years sometimes he would feel sorry and apologize.

During that bad night I assessed my situation. I was alone, with no one to turn to. Philip and my job were gone. Grandpa was dead; my only friends were people like Eunice Clark who were not real friends. Martha McGahan, whom I loved, had moved to California. My marriage was a mistake. I clearly saw that I never should have married this peculiar man, yet I did not have the courage to take my suitcase and go off somewhere by myself. That would have been Miss Sandison's counsel. And where was she, dear Miss Sandison, when I needed her? Probably in the British Museum working on Arthur Gorges.

Yet in reality nothing is as bad as it seems (or as, in logic, it ought to be). That badly injured marriage lasted seven more years, though it is true that it never recovered.